Helen: A Courtship
and
Mississippi Poems

Helen: A Courtship
and
Mississippi Poems

by
WILLIAM FAULKNER

Introductory Essays
by
Carvel Collins and Joseph Blotner

PUBLISHED JOINTLY BY
Tulane University AND Yoknapatawpha Press

Published jointly by
Yoknapatawpha Press, Box 248, Oxford, MS 38655
and Tulane University, New Orleans, Louisiana 70118

Copyright 1981 by Jill Faulkner Summers
"Biographical Background for Faulkner's *Helen*" © 1981 by Carvel Collins
"Introduction to *Mississippi Poems*" © 1981 by Joseph Blotner

All rights reserved. No part of this book may be reproduced, by any means, without permission in writing from the publisher, except by a reviewer who wishes to quote brief excerpts in connection with a review in a magazine or newspaper.

ISBN 0-916242-12-1   LC81-50422

Printed in the United States of America

CONTENTS

Biographical Background For Faulkner's *Helen*
    by Carvel Collins 9

Helen: A Courtship 111

Introduction to *Mississippi Poems*
    by Joseph Blotner 131

Mississippi Poems 149

Verse Old and Nascent: A Pilgrimage 163

Helen: A Courtship

Faulkner in New Orleans, 1925

BIOGRAPHICAL BACKGROUND FOR FAULKNER'S *HELEN*

by Carvel Collins

As a gift for Helen Baird, William Faulkner hand-lettered sixteen of his poems and bound them into the little book which he titled *Helen: A Courtship* and dated from Oxford, Mississippi, in June, 1926. She and Faulkner had met in 1925. He had fallen in love and asked her to marry him. In 1927 she married Guy Campbell Lyman. That association overtly affected at least four of Faulkner's lesser works: the fiction concerning Elmer Hodge which he began writing in 1925; *Mayday*, his January, 1926, hand-lettered gift booklet of fiction for Helen Baird; *Helen: A Courtship* (1926), containing some of the best of the poetry from which he fortunately turned toward fiction during the time he first knew her; and *Mosquitoes* (1927), his second novel, dedicated to Helen and containing a character somewhat based on her. His unsuccessful courtship of Helen in the middle of the nineteen-twenties and the friendly association Faulkner maintained for several years afterward with her and her husband had a profound effect on another work, *The Wild Palms* (1939), which in recent years many readers have come to consider one of his good novels.

Because Faulkner's relationship with Helen Baird had direct and indirect effects on his writings it deserves examination in spite of the difficulty of gathering pertinent information about it. That the difficulty is sizable becomes clear upon examining the reports of the relationship which have been published in the books and one article which so far have described it: Joseph Blotner, *Faulkner: A Biography* (1974),[1] and *Selected Letters of William Faulkner* (1977);[2] Cleanth Brooks, "The Image of Helen Baird in Faulkner's Early Fiction" (1977),[3] and *William Faulkner: Toward Yoknapatawpha and Beyond* (1978);[4] Judith Bryant Wittenberg, *Faulkner: The Transfiguration of Biography* (1979);[5] and David Minter, *William Faulkner: His Life and Work* (1980).[6]

Several elements of the relationship between Faulkner and Helen Baird cause trouble for those studies. Two among them are the amount of time Faulkner spent with her, and her opinion of him. The studies overestimate the time Faulkner was with her before she married Guy Lyman and, I believe, give no consideration to the time he spent with her husband and her in the years between their marriage and his completion of *The Wild Palms*. The difficulty those studies have with Helen Baird's opinion of Faulkner is that they estimate it to have been very low.

Faulkner and Helen Baird saw each other some at New Orleans in early 1925 and were together more frequently at the Gulf Coast town of Pascagoula, Mississippi, during much of June, 1925. But the studies which discuss their relationship say that Faulkner and Helen Baird were at Pascagoula together during the next summer as well:

> That summer of 1926 the accommodations were considerably better . . . Bill Faulkner was ready to take up his relationship with Helen Baird where he had left off the previous year . . . Pascagoula was changing. But Bill Faulkner found that nothing seemed to have changed between Helen and himself. They would go sailing, together and in groups . . . They would lie on the jetties, and he would tell her stories. They would sit at night on the swings of porches . . . He made a little book for her . . . which may have grown from stories told on those sunny

afternoons. He gave it the title . . . "Mayday" . . . Helen Baird was no longer an avid reader . . . The truth was that she appeared only to tolerate him . . . If she was not especially impressed by the poems or by *Mayday*, he would write something else. He began . . . *Mosquitoes* . . . (*F: A Biog* 508, 510–512)

[At Pascagoula in the summer of 1926, Faulkner] *spent time . . . with the neighboring Baird family—young Helen and her brothers . . . He finished his allegorical novelette,* Mayday, *and presented a copy to Helen Baird together with a booklet of sonnets.* (*Selected Letters* 32–33)

. . . Faulkner was able to see something of Helen there . . . during the summer of 1926, while he was at work writing his second novel . . . In the summer of 1926 Faulkner presented another small book to Helen. It is entitled *To [sic] Helen: A Courtship* . . . The text consists of fifteen sonnets, only five of which have been printed . . . (*W.F.: Toward Yok* 52; same information is in "Image of H.B." 220)

The summer of 1926 Faulkner spent in Pascagoula, where he divided his time between futile pursuit of a young woman and hard work on the manuscript of *Mosquitoes* . . . Helen barely tolerated him. (*F: The Transfig* 51)

As summer [1926] approached, Faulkner decided to go back to Pascagoula . . . Helen Baird was in Pascagoula, and he still hoped to impress her. They swam and boated, walked and talked. (*W.F.: His L&W* 60)

Actually Helen Baird was not at Pascagoula in the summer of 1926. She had gone to Europe. The travel diary of a Pascagoula resident records 1926 meetings with Helen and her mother at Venice, Brussels, and Paris. Helen's aunt, Martha F.

Martin, who first told me Helen was not in Pascagoula that summer, had a reason to remember 1926 with precision: The Martin family's regular house at Pascagoula burned in 1926 so they spent the summer that year in a small cottage. It was separated from where Faulkner lived by a lot empty except for the remains of their burned house. Mrs. Martin saw him often; they went to the movies together once or twice; her young son became a fan of Faulkner's; and Faulkner sometimes talked with her about his disappointment when Estelle Oldham married Cornell Franklin and about his love for her absent niece, one time quite dramatically. As further evidence, Faulkner's fragmentary draft of a letter to Helen, surviving on the back of a sheet in the *Mosquitoes* typescript which he was writing at Pascagoula during the summer of 1926, speaks of a group of poems, surely *Helen: A Courtship*: "I have made you another book . . . sonnets I wrote you, all bound."[7] *Helen: A Courtship* is dated "OXFORD-MISSISSIPPI-JUNE 1926," before Faulkner went to Pascagoula that year. The fragmentary draft letter written in Pascagoula makes clear that he had not yet been able to give the booklet to her. He did give it to her later, possibly in the winter of 1926–27, though perhaps *Helen* was the gift of holograph poems which one friend of hers told me Helen Baird accepted from Faulkner the day she married Guy Lyman, May 4, 1927. As for the published suggestion that Faulkner had presented *Helen* to her in the previous summer, 1925,[8] he could not have done so, for besides writing June, 1926, as the date of the booklet, he dated eight of the poems after his departure for Europe in July, 1925, and accompanied those dates by names of places from that trip. As for the prose gift booklet *Mayday*: Faulkner had put it together some months before the summer of 1926, dating it January 27, 1926, and probably had given it to Helen Baird before she left for Europe in February.

Helen's attitude toward Faulkner is significant enough in relation to *The Wild Palms* to warrant attention later in this es-

1926 canceled fragment draft letter by Faulkner for Helen Baird, on back of page 269 in Mosquitoes *typescript (Courtesy: University of Virginia Library)* say. But here one point can illustrate the difficulty it has presented to the published studies which discuss the relationship of Helen and Faulkner. Five of them consider a remark about *Mosquitoes* which Helen is reported to have made to a close friend in 1927 to be a significant demonstration that her opinion of Faulkner was low, even, in some of the studies, bordering on contempt:

> When Ann Farnsworth read that *Mosquitoes* had been published, she told Helen, "I see Bill Faulkner has a new book out."
> "Don't read it," Helen replied. "It's no good." (*F: A Biog* 549)

> ... Helen had advised her friend Ann Farnsworth not to read *Mosquitoes* because "It's no good" ... (*W.F.: Toward Yok* 57; same report in "Image of H.B." 230)

> [Helen] repudiated his book [*Mosquitoes*] along with his person, telling a friend, "Don't read it, it's no good" ... (*F: The Transfig* 51)

> Even his literary gifts she judged negligible. Don't bother reading *Mosquitoes*, she told a friend after Faulkner had dedicated it to her, "It's no good." (*W.F.: His L&W* 60)

That statement caused a feeling of shame for my performance as an interviewer, for I had talked with Ann Farnsworth a few times and had corresponded with her often without ever eliciting any recollection of that hostile remark about *Mosquitoes*. Admiring her intelligence and scholarly training, I recently have written her to learn more. Promptly and firmly she has replied concerning the statement that Helen told her *Mosquitoes* was no good, "This is not so."

To return to the matter of how much time Faulkner was in the presence of Helen Baird: After he had spent the spring of 1925 at work on his first novel, he and she both were at Pascagoula in June, but he was not free to devote quite so much time to courtship as the following published accounts suggest:

> By May 25 . . . Except for minor revisions to come, he had completed his first novel . . . Faulkner would finish the editing of his typescript and then it would have to be retyped. Since he knew he could count on Phil Stone, the logical thing was to send it to Oxford to be typed. He decided, apparently, to take it there himself . . . He was entitled to loaf . . . Bill Faulkner may have decided on his return to Oxford in that late spring of 1925 that he did not want to spend the summer there . . . Stone asked his sister-in-law . . . to invite Bill Faulkner down to Pascagoula to the summer place she and Jack Stone had there, and he accepted . . . With the novel finished he had gone back to poetry . . . As June began to draw to an end . . . Helen Baird and Ann Farnsworth left with their mothers to travel in France and Italy. Back in Oxford, Grace Hudson had worked long and carefully on the typescript of the novel. In Pascagoula, the author packed . . . and rode the train into the early summer heat of north Mississippi. (*F: A Biog* 430–31, 433, 439)

> After Faulkner finished the manuscript in mid-1925, he left New Orleans and went to Pascagoula . . . (*F: The Transfig* 49)

> In late May, when Faulkner finished it . . . Phil Stone could help him get the manuscript typed . . . [He] packed his manuscript, and left . . . Although Estelle Franklin was still in Oxford, Helen Baird, a woman Faulkner had met in New Orleans, was in Pascagoula. Leaving Phil to supervise the typing and Estelle to care for her two children, Faulkner joined Helen in Pascagoula, where he could swim and sail . . . Reciting Swinburne and Housman to Helen . . . he waited for Phil's secretary to finish his manuscript.

Soon he was writing poems . . . for Helen . . . To her mother . . . he seemed disreputable and presumptuous. Toward the end of June, Mrs. Baird took her daughter and left for Europe, adding her name to the list of disapproving parents. (*W.F.: His L&W* 54)

Faulkner did not finish *Soldiers' Pay* in May, 1925. He had more than minor revisions to make and actually did not complete his next-to-final rewriting and his retyping until near the end of June, at Pascagoula.

About May 21 at New Orleans he had finished his first draft of the novel, writing around 10,000 words on the marathon final day, having averaged about 3,000 on working days before that. He was reporting this progress in the correspondence he had from New Orleans with various people—including four women, in Arkansas, Mississippi, Tennessee, and Oklahoma. To the woman in Tennessee in an undated letter almost surely sent soon after April 23, he had spoken of having written more than 50,000 words of his novel. The next month when he had finished the first draft he felt disappointed to have come to the end because writing that first novel had brought a joy he might never feel again. To get a brief rest before he began what he apparently then thought would be mostly just retyping to make a clean copy for the publisher, he took a three-day cruise on a commercial boat. After that he apparently rewrote for about a week in New Orleans and then, telling them he wanted to get away from the novel for a while, asked New Orleans friends to do some of the retyping while he went out of the city. Lillian Friend Marcus, of the *Double Dealer* magazine and later to be partially the basis for the character of Eva Wiseman in *Mosquitoes*, told me she typed about two chapters. Another acquaintance who was willing to help lived in the same building as Faulkner, at 624 Orleans Alley, now Pirates Alley. The ground floor had two rooms which the resident responsible for the entire house sublet to roomers. Faulkner rented the front room and a man who worked in newspaper advertising rented the other, sharing a ground floor kitchen. The Sherwood Andersons had loaned Faulkner a cot and bedding. The other ground floor roomer greatly admired Faulkner's talent—so much, in fact, that later, when Faulkner, jettisoning weight for his travels, no longer wanted several manuscripts and typescripts, he preserved them so that now almost all are in the Berg Collection at the New York Public Library. He offered to join the retyping effort and to enlist the help of a friend.

Leaving these volunteers at work, Faulkner made a hurried trip to Oxford. According to Phil Stone he had no intention of either staying more than a few days or having his unready typescript at that time completely retyped in Oxford as final setting copy for the printers. After about five days at Oxford he left for Pascagoula, Jack Stone having invited him weeks before to visit with his family there when summer came. Faulkner did not leave Phil Stone to supervise any typing; they left Oxford together, stopping in Memphis on June 5 to visit with Dot Wilcox and Bea Stevenson, a girl friend of Phil's, and signing copies of Faulkner's first book, *The Marble Faun*. The copy to Dot Wilcox, which she discussed during one of several conversations and is in the excellent Faulkner collection of William Boozer, bears the date "5 June 1925" in Faulkner's hand, though this meeting with her and their signing the book for her have been placed in 1927 by a biography.[9]

Reaching Pascagoula on June 6, Faulkner for the next four days was completely free to see Helen Baird as often as he could. In a small sloop loaned by a boy who had left Pascagoula for summer camp, he first learned at that time the rudiments of sailing, which came to mean a great deal to him, literally for the rest of his life because the last project he was working on in Mississippi before his unexpected death was preparation for the removal of his sloop, *Ring Dove*, from the lake at Sardis to another lake a few miles south.

At New Orleans on June 11 his volunteers gave him what they had typed. Taken aback by retyping errors and how much remained to be changed in the novel, he carried it to Pascagoula and began a work schedule which though it gave him time to sail and swim and be with Helen surely gave less than he would have liked. Under pressure he finished that—apparently next-to-last—revising and retyping at Pascagoula on June 23. Judging by information from Faulkner's friends in New Orleans and Oxford and the nature of the surviving typescripts, it probably was on the last typed page of this version that Faulkner then or later wrote his holograph note, "New Orleans / May 1925,"[10] thereby, if that is so, undoubtedly causing bibliographical arguments yet to come; but detailed discussion of that concerns *Soldiers' Pay*, not *Helen*.

It is not true that Helen Baird's mother, as reported among the biographical passages quoted above, took her daughter off to Europe near the end of June, 1925. Their trip did not begin until months later. But Faulkner certainly left Pascagoula without hope for a favorable outcome of his proposal of marriage.

He returned to Oxford but could stay less than a week, for he was committed to accompanying William Spratling on a freighter bound for Italy, the *West Ivis*, with which Spratling, contrary to his recollections many years later, had made the arrangements for them both to go as paying passengers.

After the freighter's arrival at New Orleans behind schedule, they finally sailed on July 7. It was Faulkner's intention, as letters in Phil Stone's files make clear, to stay abroad for a fairly long time, more than long enough for there to be some chance that he might meet Helen Baird when she reached Europe late the next winter. Thoughts of that possibility inform parts of the *Elmer* manuscripts he worked on in Paris. But that meeting was not to be, for by November, 1925, Faulkner was ready to come home. A few weeks later he finally did leave France and, as he reported at once in a letter sending messages back to three Paris friends, reached New York on

December 19. Surely to his surprise, he found Helen Baird there. She was in the city to explore possibilities for marketing her dolls and figures, which she was already successfully selling through some of the Vieux Carré shops. She told me that she was put out by Faulkner's shabby appearance, which she attributed to his having been on a walking tour. Perhaps it was due more to his uncomfortable ocean crossing, which he graphically reported in the letter to Paris. A contributing element may have been the full beard he had grown abroad, which Helen never saw before or after that December meeting. It was probably just as well that their visits to Paris did not coincide, for that would have dramatized further the differences between their financial conditions and prospects: When Helen and her mother did reach Paris they stayed briefly at a hotel in the rue Jacob. Then Helen's mother, wanting her to have the advantages of a better hotel, moved them to the George V, considered at that time the city's best. Faulkner too stayed at a hotel in the rue Jacob when he first reached Paris in 1925, but before long, with the help of a friend, lugged his baggage up the hill to cheaper quarters in the rue Servandoni. In deference to whatever human hopes or sympathies caused the large sales of Horatio Alger's books, one should point out here that in later years Mrs. Baird, according to her daughter, read Faulkner's works saying, "He really can string words together," and after he received the Nobel Prize, Faulkner sometimes chose to stay at the George V.

This seems to be the place, while discussing a few of the innumerable and documentable misconceptions about Faulkner's biography, to point out in a kind of parenthesis that mistakes about Faulkner's life are easy to make and that I know it to my sorrow, having made more than enough. It is impossible to avoid all errors in biographical writing about anyone, but the possibilities for error sharply increase when the subject of the biography is, like William Faulkner, adamantly opposed to having a book about his or her life ever published.

With Faulkner, one of the additional special problems is that when study of his extremely complex and sophisticated works first began, much literary criticism was so dominated by simplistic principles that anyone owning a typewriter felt ready to judge and propagandize favorably or unfavorably about his novels with extreme self-confidence and no sense of the necessity for serious examination. By now many excellent published critical studies have been guiding readers into better understanding of Faulkner's writing, but in biographical studies some of the original unjustified self-confidence and lack of concern for evidence remain. An experienced Faulkner specialist has jokingly suggested that the enormous amount of inaccuracy put into print about Faulkner's life since his death may be from a curse, a supernatural continuation of Faulkner's passionate desire never to have his biography written.

While discussing the errors of others it is embarrassing to think of the biographical errors I have published, the closeness of some of the near misses, and the probability of publishing new errors—in this essay, for example. Years ago while discussing the popular misconception that Faulkner had joined a Canadian military air service in 1918, I put in print that he had joined the Royal Flying Corps. Actually the name had changed to Royal Air Force before he joined, but too inexperienced to do the easy but essential pessimistic checking, I trapped myself by Faulkner's frequent references to his serving in the R.F.C., by the words "Royal Flying Corps" on his uniform, and by the metal R.F.C. insignia his mother showed me. Soon after, in trying for correction of the error, I perpetrated a new one when printers, disregarding abject marginal pleading, put initial capitals on all three words of "British air force," creating a new, never-existent organization and further irritating a segment of the Faulkner industry.

For years in publicly discussing Quentin's section of *The Sound and the Fury* I said it was pertinent that Faulkner perhaps saw the elaborate 1925 Corpus Christi procession which a Sherwood Anderson letter describes as moving out from the cathedral across the narrow street from Faulkner's New Orleans room. In preparing this essay I have realized Faulkner had gone back to Pascagoula two days before that event. Further demonstration of glass house residency and further support for the specialist's joke that Faulkner perhaps put a curse on biographical accuracy have appeared while this piece is being prepared for the printers. A review of the just-published original version of *Sanctuary* contains a statement which is repeated and featured in a box at the center of the review's first page:

> "'Sanctuary' was based on a story that Faulkner had heard from a woman in a New Orleans nightclub about her abduction by an impotent gangster." [11]

That boxed statement stems not from the book being reviewed but from information in a one-page essay which I contributed to a *Harvard Advocate* early all-Faulkner issue, in November of 1951. That brief essay, the result of interviews with several people including the woman Faulkner had overheard, makes no mention of "abduction" or "New Orleans," which the review has added without evidence. There actually was no abduction in what Faulkner overheard being said by the woman, a competent professional prostitute who had been glad to get work. When Faulkner overheard her telling her tale he was in Memphis, not New Orleans. Surely a small matter, but mentioned here because having got out that old *Advocate* essay to see whether it had been misleading about abduction and New Orleans I see it said *Sanctuary* had been "remunerative," which is untrue. The novel's large publicity and sales had made that seem a good idea at the time; two years later I learned, like everyone else interested in Faulkner, that because of his publishers' financial difficulties *Sanctuary* was by no means remunerative for him.

When Helen Baird and William Faulkner met, she had lived most of her life in Nashville, Tennessee. Her father was the president and editor of an influential and profitable trade journal, *The Southern Lumberman*. He was just completing the construction of a very large house in 1915 when he was killed by a train while walking to the terminal exits from a Pullman car, which had been parked in the railway yards for the passengers' comfort after its early morning arrival at

Helen Baird and her mother, Nashville

Nashville. He was survived by his wife and four children: Helen, about ten years of age, youngest, and three sons. Mrs. Baird maintained a vacation house at the beach in Pascagoula, where her children spent much time. During the earlier half of 1925 when Faulkner was in New Orleans Helen was there for a while. As a resident of the French Quarter said, she was one of the uptown people who often came to the Quarter "partly slumming among the odd and interesting artistic types." That resident and others liked her, finding her "fun" and "very outspoken." Ann Farnsworth, one of her closest friends, says that Helen struck people as vivacious, intelligent, and vibrant, and was "extremely attractive but not beautiful." William B. Wisdom said she had "an elfin quality" which was very appealing. (John McClure, one of the founders of the *Double Dealer*, editor in those years of a highly regarded book page in the *Times-Picayune*, and Faulkner's friend, used the same phrase about Faulkner, telling me that Faulkner then had "an elfin quality which struck me as unusual.") Mr. and Mrs. Marc Antony remembered Helen in the Quarter in the middle of the nineteen-twenties as "pixy," "plumpish," and "attractive."

She fell in love with Guy Lyman and married him. Obviously Faulkner was in no financial or career position to marry and start supporting a wife when he was barely supporting himself. But it is doubtful that Helen Baird found him so unlikable as the published accounts of their association suggest. In a letter of November 29, 1951, she told me she thought Faulkner "one grand person to know and be with—a truly great companion like the ones you read about but never meet." In a conversation later she told my wife and me that Faulkner's proposal of marriage was a significant matter to her. One friend of Helen's has even gone so far as to say that she was "crazy about him." Whatever the fact was, it does seem wrong, as an example, for an opinion reported to have been expressed by her mother—that the pipe-smoking Faulkner smelled—to be converted by a later biography into a statement that Helen herself thought him "smelly."

Certainly he was no sartorial paragon at Pascagoula. Helen's mother's sister, Mrs. Martin, who liked him, said that when Faulkner arrived he gave the appearance of "a bird who just flew in from the trees." He was, she said, extremely thin and he was ragged with his hair quite long. Her niece told me Faulkner had said that when he was younger he much of the time dressed almost foppishly; Mrs. Martin said he not only had told her that but had gone on to explain: After he lost Estelle Oldham he quit caring how he dressed. Enjoying the freedom of the beach and dedicated to romantic self images, he went barefoot at a time when it was not respectable. Perhaps using a rope to support his white ducks made him look, in Melville's words about Babo's similar belt, "like a begging friar of St. Francis," a saint whom Faulkner admired; but when asked why he used the piece of rope, he courteously explained: He liked it.

Ann Farnsworth remembers that Faulkner, white duck trousers, bare feet, and mustache, was regarded as "quite a character." And he did not help his respectability by becoming the friend of a fully certified local character, a man well acquainted with the Mississippi country back from the beach, who irritated the genteel by going barefoot, with his toes sticking far out—apparently remarkably far, for some residents of Pascagoula allege he had six on each foot; Faulkner could only emulate not equal. Perhaps his new friendship gave Faulkner thoughts of the special-footed amphibious members of Al Jackson's family in the tall tales he and Sherwood Anderson had worked up, had even decided enthusiastically near the end of March, 1925, to make into a book consciously modeled somewhat on Harris's Sut Lovingood *Yarns* and to use the royalties to buy a boat in partnership. But by this second summer at Pascagoula Faulkner seems to have become aware of the boredom of most tall tales when presented in much quantity, for as he wrote along in *Mosquitoes* he made the Anderson-based character, Dawson Fairchild, persistently bore the groaning people of the boating party with Al Jackson tales until Eva Wiseman acted in the interest of all: "'Dawson' she said firmly, 'shut up. We simply cannot stand any more.'"

It is interestingly inconsistent that Faulkner, whose bare feet and white ducks were objects of disparagement by the Pascagoula establishment in the summers of 1925 and 1926, would speak disparagingly during the winter which fell between them—in his December, 1925, letter to Paris describing his Atlantic crossing—about the bare feet of many of the immigrant passengers and the white duck pants of one of them.

Faulkner told Mrs. Martin he never let his mother throw away his old clothing, and she believed him. But in respect for her he dressed neatly when they went to the movies. She was intelligent, humorous, frank, and, in addition to liking Faulkner personally, valued the judgment of her very young son, Edward, who "became absolutely devoted" to Faulkner in what she observed to be a "man-to-man" friendship. She was touched that Faulkner obviously had great ambition as a writer but no one paid much attention then to his writing. She was quite willing to listen as Faulkner talked to her, in the summer of 1926, about his feelings for her absent niece. And Faulkner noted those talks with her not only in a much later letter to Helen but while he was in the midst of them and writing *Mosquitoes*, in which Gordon, the Patricia-smitten sculptor, talks about Patricia to her fictional aunt, Mrs. Maurier—a character, by the way, who in none of the elements of her unlucky personality was modeled on Mrs. Martin.

The Elmer Hodge materials—which include the unfinished novel, *Elmer*, that Faulkner worked on after he left New Orleans for Europe in 1925; one story he completed later;[12] and his partial attempts at other stories[13]—contain much which Faulkner would develop with great success in his fiction. But here it is necessary to leave aside those interesting "loomings" and discuss only the elements in *Elmer* which seem to grow out of Faulkner's having fallen unsuccessfully in love with Helen Baird. Elmer Hodge, without money or prospects, falls in love with oil-rich Myrtle Monson in Houston and blurts out an ineffective proposal of marriage. Myrtle, with her mother, leaves for Europe. Faulkner additionally links Elmer to himself by such an early detail as the fictional screwdriver which Elmer had kept in his childhood treasure box and the real screwdriver which Faulkner's mother told me had been among his most valued possessions as a child. The Elmer papers also report that Elmer had returned from World War training "interesting and limping" and using a walking stick —as Faulkner had done. More nearly current, 1925, autobiography includes the Atlantic freighter crossing to Europe seeking development as an artist; William Spratling's arrest in Genoa (changed to Elmer's in Venice); Faulkner's moving from a better Paris hotel to the one in the rue Servandoni and Elmer's doing the same, street name and all; and significant memories of a loved girl who had married a more established young man (an Ethel for Elmer, Estelle Oldham for Faulkner). Elmer hopes to see Myrtle and Mrs. Monson in Europe, and Faulkner at first expected still to be in Europe when Helen and Mrs. Baird arrived. Elmer seems to have problems with Mrs. Monson's social aspirations as Faulkner was to tell Helen's aunt, Martha Martin, he felt he had with Mrs. Baird's, a theme which appears elsewhere in Faulkner's life and works: He also was to tell Mrs. Martin that he felt it was chiefly Mrs. Oldham's desire for her daughter to have a financially and socially established husband which had caused Estelle Oldham in 1918 to marry Cornell Franklin instead of himself; and in *The Sound and the Fury*, the plot of which Faulkner told to a Paris friend in the same months he was first at work on *Elmer*, Mrs. Compson's concern for social status is a major factor in the overwhelming of her family.

Elmer's fictional father's good luck with an oil well—indicated by some of the Elmer papers and also mentioned by Faulkner in 1925 to Sibleigh and other Paris friends—gives Elmer the money to study art in Europe and again see Myrtle, whom he holds in his mind in romantic image.

Some of the least interesting parts of the unfinished *Elmer* concern Myrtle Monson and her mother, who often appear as a satire on the American female traveler, and who become involved with fortune-hunting British aristocrats in a large section of the novel which fails. Like the section of *Redburn* in which Melville's protagonist leaves ship and Liverpool docks for an unconvincing foray into posh gambling at London, perhaps Faulkner's British aristocracy material, in spite of the successful humor in a small part of it, fails because the author does not know what he is talking about.

One can speculate that much of the Monson material in *Elmer* is dull because Faulkner seems to have used it too bluntly as a way of exorcising the frustration of his disappointed love for Helen Baird. By maintaining very little aesthetic distance while denigrating the Monsons in *Elmer*, Faulkner may have eased more quickly some of his pain about Helen, a method he knew from experience to be effective, having used it before in much cruder form. Though published biography says that between Estelle Oldham's marriage in 1918 and his falling in love with Helen Baird in 1925 Faulkner had no significant love interest, he actually had one of considerable significance to him. To quote from an introduction I supplied for the publication of *Mayday*:

> Some years before, between 1919 and 1922, Faulkner had fallen in love with a young woman at Charleston, Mississippi, where he often went to visit Phil Stone while Stone was working there in one of his family's law offices. When she did not respond to Faulkner's affection he felt considerable emotional distress. But he cured himself, he

told Stone, by deliberately developing mental pictures of that otherwise idealized person engaged in the least romantic regularly repeated acts of our species.[14]

Though the apparent delay in timing raises questions, the frustration of that earlier love may have been the cause of the extreme emotional disturbance Faulkner experienced during the spring of 1924 and reported in a letter from Oxford to a Mississippi friend about five months later, saying that he was just recovering and once again able to write. He hoped the powers that be would prevent his having another such ordeal. If that painful emotional experience really was the result of his frustrated love at Charleston which Phil Stone described to me, Faulkner's hope to avoid another was not to be fulfilled: unfortunately for him but fortunately for readers of *The Wild Palms*, within a few months he was to fall hopelessly in love with Helen Baird.

In *Elmer* the voice of the author tells us more than once that Elmer, misled by infatuation, does not realize the shortcomings of his beloved, and that not only is Myrtle now personally and physically less than Elmer's idealization of her but in the near future she will become physically even less ideal. He supports this prediction by having Myrtle angrily—"damn damn damn"—observe physical changes in herself. In *Elmer*, to serve Faulkner's need, the unattainable grapes are sour.

In writing *Mayday*, the allegorical novelette which he bound as a gift for Helen Baird and dated in January of 1926, Faulkner was not hostile to the unattainable beloved as he had been in *Elmer*. He did not try at all to create for his personal relief a less idealized conception of Helen. The way he seems to have attempted in *Mayday* to reduce the pain of his frustrated love is much more general. He showed that all idealized love is frustrated: The protagonist, Sir Galwyn of Arthgyle, a young knight, has love affairs with three desirable women, including the bride of King Mark of Cornwall, Yseult. But the affairs are extremely brief—by Galwyn's choice. Once attained, the women, though legendary in beauty and desirability, cannot hold his interest.

Faulkner drew some aspects of this cynical theme from James Branch Cabell, who then was highly regarded. His works often stress that every ideal love is unattainable because, even when lover wins beloved, the ideal fades into reality. Though Faulkner used several of Cabell's other writings as well, he based much of *Mayday* on *Jurgen* which was famous then because of its 1922 obscenity trial.[15] Other Cabell works quite possibly contributed variously: *The Line of Love*, the twisting of the first day of May from happiness to disappointment; *Figures of Earth*, the term "designs" for the allegorical figures Hunger and Pain which ride beside Galwyn, and the "dark stream of Lethe" which ends the novel just as the "dark hurrying stream" ends *Mayday*; *Domnei*, for its reinforcement of the idea that if passion is not sublimated time will destroy the loved image; *The High Place: A Comedy of Disenchantment*, perhaps for the tone indicated by its subtitle, its repetition of the Cabellian boredom after the unattainable has been attained, and its account of "nympholepts" (of which more later); and *The Rivet in Grandfather's Neck*, for its reinforcement of the troubadours' concept of a "love which rather abhors than otherwise the notion of possessing its object."

But Faulkner in *Mayday* departs from Cabell in a significant way: Cabell's protagonists—Jurgen, Michael, and others—almost invariably come to accept and adjust and so live on, but Faulkner's Sir Galwyn drowns himself. Like much of *Mayday*, this is tightly connected to Quentin Compson's section of *The Sound and the Fury*, one of Faulkner's masterpieces on which he was already at work,[16] but it also relates to Faulkner's early and unusually strong concern with death, to be discussed later while examining the poems in *Helen: A Courtship*. One aspect of it should be mentioned here. The fact that death is a main element of *Mayday* has confused some readers. One published piece of criticism assumes that the girl—"all young and red and white, and with long shining hair like a column of fair sunny water"—whose image Galwyn sees in the "hurrying dark waters" during a vision at the start of the novelette is Galwyn's ideal earthly love, and that at the end of the novelette Galwyn sees the image of a different girl in the stream and learns from Saint Francis that she is "Little sister Death." He then kills himself by joining her in the water because, that critical work assumes, he has learned that his ideal girl of the original vision is unattainable.[17]

Actually there are not two different girls in the "hurrying water," only one: Sister Death. It is to her image that Galwyn is drawn from the beginning—in Faulkner's dramatization of the close relationship between Eros and Thanatos which the spread of Freud's ideas on the subject in the literary world had brought into the conversation of Faulkner's New Orleans acquaintances, and presumably into his reading, by 1925. (Here as elsewhere Faulkner demonstrated remarkable ability to take from the published work of others anything useful to his fiction even when he disliked those works. He published objections to Freud in the 1920s but here in *Mayday* as earlier, with some intentional crudity, in *Elmer* and later, with subtle effectiveness, in *The Sound and the Fury* he used some of Freud's ideas. Similarly in *Elmer* he used material partly influenced by Flaubert's *The Temptation of St. Anthony* though while in France and trying to get on with *Elmer* he wrote in his copy of *The Temptation* an astonishing, emotional attack against the book, additionally astonishing because years later he gave the book extreme praise. Though he wrote in 1925 that he did not admire Huxley's *Those Barren Leaves*, he quite soon drew on it extensively for *Mosquitoes*.) Perhaps one reason that piece of criticism does not get the point of *Mayday* is that it elsewhere says Faulkner possibly had not read "a great deal" of Freud.[18] Faulkner did not need to read much to take what he used in his fiction and we would have to invoke severe academic snobbery to think that as an active, serious, and eclectic reader he would not have read any. That work of criticism goes on at once to wonder whether Faulkner expected Helen Baird to get the point of *Mayday*. It concludes that he probably did not because he dedicated the gift booklet "to thee / O wise and lovely / this: / a fumbling in darkness," and then further wonders in passing whether *Mayday* was a "fumbling in darkness" in which even Faulkner did not understand the meaning of the story. This is not Faulkner's only dedication which speaks of "fumbling" and "darkness": In 1920 he had given a copy of his hand-lettered *Marionettes* to Estelle Franklin's very young child, Victoria, possibly as an indirect way of giving it to her mother. Its dedication says in part: ". . . THIS, A SHADOWY FUMBLING IN / WINDY DARKNESS . . ." By these dedications one assumes Faulkner meant the two works were trying to explore possibly incomprehensible aspects of life—or of *his* life—not that at some modest level of difficult thought he had no idea what he was doing.

Though suicide is the final action of *Mayday*, at no time does the story of Sir Galwyn's progression to that end have the "you'll be sorry" tone in which many a frustrated lover has written about suicide to the beloved. In spite of its main subject—death—and Faulkner's unhappiness in his love for Helen Baird, *Mayday* perhaps stayed well above that level because of its close relationship to the development of *The Sound and the Fury*, in which Faulkner was to keep his various emotional involvements under full aesthetic control.

In *Mosquitoes*, which Faulkner in typescript dedicated "To Helen, Beautiful and Wise," he achieved some of that control, beyond what he had displayed in the unfinished *Elmer*. The complexity of his treatment of Patricia Robyn in *Mosquitoes* is on the way toward the much greater complexity of his treatment a decade later of Charlotte Rittenmeyer in *The Wild Palms*. Faulkner worked only briefly on *Mosquitoes* during his stay at Paris, where he wrote much of the *Elmer* material about Elmer's relationship with Myrtle Monson and her mother. Most of *Mosquitoes* he wrote in 1926. Even that modest removal in time from the first impact of Helen's unattainability may have made possible his more detached treatment of Patricia, but a larger factor may have been Faulkner's growing ability in general to use his emotional situations for the benefit of his novels rather than, as with *Elmer*, the reverse. T. S. Eliot said, "The more perfect the artist the more completely separate in him will be the man who suffers and the mind which creates."

There are additional possible reasons for the more complex treatment of Patricia Robyn. Though *Elmer* had drawn on literary works by other writers, its autobiographical elements outweigh those borrowings, but much more of *Mosquitoes* is formed by literary sources. One of Faulkner's early literary friends, in a 1925 letter to a book reviewer, remarked that Faulkner was talented and could be good but he was idiotic to be so readily influenced by the writings of others. That remark may have contained considerable truth when applied to some of Faulkner's poetry, but its applicability was to shrink rapidly as Faulkner moved along in his career. All his creative life he would make repeated and extensive use of literary sources—if often only by ironic reversal—and his readers would profit by the ways he did it. Faulkner, having read three books by Hergesheimer, published in 1922 in the University of Mississippi newspaper a review of them, which I came upon in the late 1940's and subsequently reprinted in a volume of his college writings.[19] Later, in a 1925 letter which he wrote from New Orleans to the woman in Tennessee, he mentioned two books he recently had read, one of them Huxley's *Those Barren Leaves*. It was surprising, upon going then through those works, to find how much Faulkner had used elements from Hergesheimer and Huxley to shape *Mosquitoes* even though his 1922 review had disparaged Hergesheimer as not really a novelist but "an emasculate priest surrounded by the puppets he has carved and clothed and painted" and his 1925 letter had said he considered *Those Barren Leaves* much inferior to Mottram's *The Spanish Farm*. For *Mosquitoes* Faulkner drew additionally on Huxley[20] and on other writers also, among them Eliot,[21] Joyce,[22] and Flaubert.

With such broad commitment to literary borrowings, *Mosquitoes* is less generally autobiographical than *Elmer*. But its autobiography does go beyond the basic framework of a cruise by characters partially based on identifiable people of Faulkner's New Orleans acquaintance (with several of whom it was possible to discuss their recollections of similar real cruises and their reactions to the novel). For example, he put himself in the book not only under his own name as a small dark man, who at one point compliments Jenny on her physique, but partially in David and in Gordon, both of whom are intensely drawn to Patricia Robyn. Faulkner, like everyone else, had many concepts which persisted throughout his life; in *Mosquitoes* he autobiographically gave one of them to Gordon: Drawing on Rostand's *Cyrano*, as Mary M. Dunlap pointed out some years ago,[23] Faulkner had Gordon speak of Patricia's name as "a little golden bell hung" in his heart. In Faulkner's fragment draft letter written while he worked on *Mosquitoes* he brings up the same concept, telling Helen her "name is like a little golden bell hung in my heart, dearest one." Years later he put an interesting variation into a letter to Joan Williams postmarked December 20, 1952: Faulkner mentions a little bell he hopes she will wear, and says that even if the ardor of his letter makes her run away the running will cause the bell to sound for her his name.

In *Mosquitoes* Faulkner obviously had Helen in mind for part of Patricia's characterization, for example when he gave Patricia's brother Theodore Robyn details from the real life of one of Helen's brothers: the nicknames "Josh" and "Gus" and the attempt to make a tobacco pipe of a new type. This is presented with some inaccuracy by published biography, where

Helen's brother James R. Baird, who wrote for the New Orleans *Times-Picayune* when Faulkner was at New Orleans and Pascagoula and was in reality called "Pete," is repeatedly called "Josh" and is said to have been the source for the fictional Theodore Robyn's pipe and nicknames.[24] It was another of Helen's brothers who actually worked on a pipe and was called both "Josh" and "Gus." Much more significantly, it is also untrue, according to a long-time family friend, that Helen seemed to feel any closer to one brother than to the others, an idea which has been made something of in print, probably because *Mosquitoes* is mistakenly confused with a report of reality and because that unfounded idea helps shore up tidy psycho-sexual theories which have developed. (In *Floater*—a satiric novel about news magazines by Calvin Trillin who worked for one—a writer says, "'Control over the story increases in inverse ratio to knowledge of what actually went on.'")[25] But Patricia Robyn and her situation are by no means direct importation of Helen Baird from reality into fiction.

Patricia, though her name means "noble," is an ambivalent character. She is energetic, humorous at times, independent, and attractive enough to fascinate the sculptor, Gordon, and David, the steward, and, like the admired Caddy of *The Sound and the Fury*, to make another character "conscious of the clean young odor of her, like that of young trees." She also is often selfish, too confident, naive, removed from reality, inconsiderate, and, when carried on David's back while ashore among the mosquitoes, as onerous a burden as the old man on the back of Sinbad in his fifth voyage. Her confused or undeveloped sexuality—like many of the rest of her characteristics—does not come from any model in reality but from literary purposes Faulkner needed her to serve. One theme of *Mosquitoes* is that sexuality has been corrupted; so the fictional characters Faulkner invites on the cruise form an anthology of sex defects, with none of them having a healthy and joyful sexual situation. A character who seems at first to be an exception is Jenny, the New Orleans girl Patricia brought along at the last minute. Jenny has no sexual confusions and physically is compellingly attractive. Like Faulkner's later symbols of natural fecundity—Lena Grove of *Light in August*, for example [26]—Jenny is no intellectual nor is she presented as needing to be one. The role Faulkner assigns her is to be the essence of the healthy sexuality from which the other characters are cut off.

Jenny, like Patricia, has some literary origins, but one list of the actual people partially used as characters in this *roman à clef* is not entirely correct when it reports that for Jenny there is "No identifiable real-life equivalent." Though Jenny's appearance, nature, and situation differ from those of the girl Faulkner had fallen in love with at Charleston, he revealed a glimpse of his autobiography by giving Jenny not only the initials of that girl but an almost identical last name. When even Jenny, excellently aimed and equipped for sex, cannot find a satisfactory lover among those aboard, the sexual confusion and frustration of the boating party are total. To fill out the collection of sex defects, Faulkner needed a character to represent incest and elected Patricia to demonstrate it by her extreme emotional involvement with her fictional brother Theodore, an attachment which Faulkner apparently felt he could increase by making them twins. Faulkner also gave Patricia some sexual ambiguity so her character could contribute, like the "Hermaphroditus" poem, to another theme of the novel. Patricia Robyn in *Mosquitoes* has so much work to do in fitting the character called for by Faulkner's novelistic requirements that she cannot be just an object of retaliation or disparagement as Myrtle is much of the time in *Elmer* or an object of complete devotion as Helen is in *Helen: A Courtship*.

Helen: A Courtship reports the different stages of the poet's love in a logical sequential arrangement of the sixteen poems.

Influential early criticism of Faulkner accused him of having insufficient organizing power to sustain his novels, which were therefore said to be less important than the general pattern of his fictional county's "saga." A large number of readers came to believe that, but criticism long since has moved beyond such a hampering judgment. Faulkner made no public objection to that damaging accusation of not being able to create good and sustained organization in his novels, but he privately voiced his intense resentment. He knew he was demonstrating in his best fiction a genius for structure, though often of an unconventional—and therefore more interesting—sort. He took seriously even the minor aesthetic job of arranging the collections of his shorter works for which he was allowed to determine the order. And according to his friend who showed it to me, Faulkner gave a great amount of pleasurable attention to preparing a detailed plan for a complete collected edition of his fiction if one were ever to be published. In it he not only disregarded the chronological orders of writing and publication but marched to a different beat from that of the criticism which began years ago drumming the belief that one of the important features of Faulkner's work is the chronology of his fictional county.

Helen did not call for great organizational powers, but Faulkner used his well enough to present unqualified admiration for Helen Baird. Because Faulkner had some of these sixteen poems on hand before he met her and had to fit them into his plan and write others to fill the gaps, he must have had a few organizational problems and now and then a somewhat difficult decision, but he ended with a workable sequence: The prefatory poem praises Helen, with no overtly stated involvement of the poet. The first of the sonnets reports the admirable quieting, calming effect of the beloved on the poet and is in no way sensual. The next treats sexuality in a general way, emphasizing its presence in human beings always. Spring, says the following sonnet, brings sensual, sexual delight. Then

Helen Baird

a sonnet first presents the frustration of sensual desire. In the fifth, one third through the numbered sequence, the poet imagines his desire has been fulfilled, a thought heightened by its ironic, comic contrast to his imagined dialogue with the mother of his beloved. Next is praise—by way of the poet's "fevered loud distress"—of the beloved's body in its sensual attractiveness. The seventh sonnet seems to be a somewhat harsh invocation of Horace's *carpe diem*. "Virginity" advances that theme. Sonnet IX, which I understand least of all, may mark the end of the poet's hope for complete physical union with his beloved. In sonnet X, two-thirds through the sequence, the poet tells the beloved that though she has refused to make love with him he has made love with her often in imagination. In the remaining five sonnets the poet reports that his love will continue: (XI) It is so strong that he wants no resurrection until he can forget his beloved. (XII) There will be no end to his love in this life. (XIII) His heart, separated from his beloved's, is dead "yet darkly troubled." (XIV) Grief is better than nothing; the poet must be resigned to being without his beloved. The final sonnet gives the highest praise: When, in time, "Though warm in dark between the breasts of Death," the poet says his heart, "one stubborn leaf," though it die each dawn, will come to life again each night, presumably forever. In the sonnet's probable association of night with sensuality and the leaf's life with the night, the poet ends his praise with admiring emphasis on the calm, durable power of his beloved's sensual attraction which he had not mentioned at the beginning and only slowly had moved toward in getting the sequence under way.

"To Helen, Swimming"

Of the sixteen poems in *Helen*, nine have been found published in some form even if only as a line or two, leaving seven, so far as one can tell, to be published here for the first time.

"To Helen, Swimming" is one of the latter. It is the only poem in the booklet not a sonnet, presumably because of its introductory role. Though Faulkner dated some of the sonnets unreliably, that he accurately dated this poem in June of 1925 at Pascagoula seems likely because it has a beach setting and, unlike several of the other poems in *Helen*, has no known extant earlier versions in working drafts or in holograph or typed copies.

One of the easily understood in the booklet, the poem acceptably presents the wave pattern in terms of valleys, battlements, and city. Its description of Helen Baird accords with Faulkner's conception of her as being boyish in build which he presented in his other early treatments of her. One study says:

> . . . the opening sonnet in Faulkner's *To Helen* sequence is entitled "To Helen, Swimming," and refers to "Her boy's breast and the plain flanks of a boy."
>
> When Faulkner met Helen Baird in 1925 she was twenty-one, though Pat Robyn, the character in *Mosquitoes* modeled upon her, is obviously Faulkner's conception of what she might have been like as a girl of eighteen.[27]

Mosquitoes describes Pat Robyn as having a "boy's body," and *Helen: A Courtship* describes Helen of 1925–26 in the same way. Some speculation has been printed about Faulkner's sexual orientation because his early works, among them *Soldiers' Pay*, *Elmer*, *Mosquitoes*, and the poems, included girls with boyish figures. One partial explanation could be that in the nineteen-twenties that figure was the fashion. Another possible contributing cause, as well as effect: Estelle Oldham was a slender girl and young woman. Whatever the reason and whatever that preference says about Faulkner's psychology at the time, those who have worried about it in print may be able to relax a little because over the next quarter century Faulkner's conception of the physical ideal broadened with the figures of his peers until in the '50's he said he had come to admire women who had the legs and thighs which Bouguereau chose to paint.

To remain with the anatomical: The poem's ending—"simple music of her knees"—brings to mind an attack on Faulkner's writing which the University of Mississippi newspaper printed in 1920. Apparently the first direct commentary on Faulkner ever published, it inaugurated what is now six decades of criticism. Among its other objections to Faulkner, the student's attack said, "Mr. Editor, wouldn't this be a fine University if all of us were to . . . while away our time singing of lascivious knees, smiling lute strings, and voluptuous toes?"[28] That pioneering critic's hostility had been elicited by the opening lines of Faulkner's first known published literary work, "L'Apres-Midi d'un Faune," which had appeared in *The New Republic* in August, 1919, and later was reprinted in a slightly different version by the University's newspaper: "I follow through the singing trees / Her streaming clouded hair and face / And lascivious dreaming knees / Like gleaming water . . ." As during the rest of his career in all matters, Faulkner in this minor one did not let criticism deter him from putting what he wanted into his writing: Admirable knees were to appear again, not only here but farther along this sonnet sequence in V and VI, and elsewhere.

I "Bill"

Like the introductory poem, this first sonnet has never been published, and no work sheets or earlier versions of it have turned up. Its first stanza reminds one of statements Faulkner made in a prose sketch he wrote early in 1925 for the New Orleans *Times-Picayune*, "Out of Nazareth." There he said of his artist friend Spratling that his "hand has been shaped to a brush as mine has (alas!) not" and later in the sketch said of himself that "words are my meat and bread and drink."[29]

Early in his life Faulkner had begun to draw and paint. The first known publication by him is a drawing in the University of Mississippi's 1917 annual. One of his teachers recalled that in high school Faulkner had made interesting drawings, and Faulkner's friend and fellow student, Myrtle Ramey Demarest, preserved some of his high school drawings and generously loaned them several years ago. Faulkner put drawings and three watercolors in *Mayday*, the other booklet he gave to Helen Baird, and illustrated additional booklets, including *Marionettes* (1920) and *The Lilacs* (1920). Obviously, though, judging by "Out of Nazareth" and this poem, he had fully realized by 1925 that his art would be writing.

Continuing to speak biographically about these poems, one can speculate that the second stanza of this one partly reflects Faulkner's awareness of the deficiencies of his earliest apprentice writing. In 1921 he had spoken disparagingly to Katherine Lawless about the long poem *The Marble Faun*, some time before he published it as his first book. He tried to move beyond that work's sterile pastoral posturings in his subsequent poems, sometimes with fair success, for example in this sonnet's final stanza of loving praise for Helen.

Faulkner's use of the word "flame" in line 13 of this sonnet and elsewhere in works associated with Helen Baird will be discussed later, in connection with *The Wild Palms*.

II.

Faulkner wrote versions of this second sonnet before the June, 1925, date he gave to it in *Helen*. Typescript versions first became available in the early 'fifties when three appeared among the few hundred variously charred Faulkner papers from the debris of Phil Stone's house when I spread them out to dry on his lawn about ten years after the fire. One of them showed a title, "Sonnet." Each presented a slightly different version. Faulkner had dated one December, 1924. I believe all three are now at the Humanities Research Center of the University of Texas. In the Berg Collection is a typescript Faulkner had with him at New Orleans—fittingly titled "March," the month of strong winds, and dated December 15, 1924—which oddly enough differs a little from the typescript bearing that title and the same date which Myrtle Ramey Demarest kindly made available some years ago. Faulkner had given it to her in 1924 as part of a group titled *Mississippi Poems*, which recently has been acquired by L. D. Brodsky and published as a first-edition facsimile in 1979 by the Yoknapatawpha Press with an introduction by Joseph Blotner. Faulkner himself published an untitled version of the poem in 1933 as XLII in *A Green Bough*.

Except for that one in *A Green Bough*, all versions I have seen generally agree with lines 5 and 6 of the version in *Helen* when they speak in various ways of man's keeping warm on cold nights by "Expiating" or getting "pardon" or "forgiveness" for old "sins he did commit." In *A Green Bough* XLII Faulkner changed it to "Regretting olden sins he did omit," making that version accord with his later statement that he had realized long ago one regrets not what one did but what one did not do.

A more significant difference is in line 9. Earlier and later versions than the one in *Helen* say that "old gods fall away," but the line in *Helen* II says "new gods fall away." Lewis P. Simpson in "Sex & History: Origins of Faulkner's Apocrypha" has written:

> Perhaps I can get most directly into the early perception of the nexus of sex and history in Faulkner by referring to one of his irregular Italian sonnets. Written before 1925, possibly in 1924, this poem is numbered XLII in *A Green Bough*. (Although not published until 1933, this volume collects poems written during Faulkner's poetic period several years earlier.) The octave of the sonnet (rhymed in

the Shakespearean rather than the Italian style) interprets the symbolism of the story of the Hebraic Garden of Eden in a literal way.

> Beneath the apple tree Eve's tortured shape
> Glittered in the Snake's, her riven breast
> Sloped his coils and took the sun's escape
> To augur black her sin from east to west.
> In winter's night man may keep him warm
> Regretting olden sins he did omit;
> With fetiches the whip of blood to charm,
> Forgetting that with breath he's heir to it.

The sestet expands and comments on the theme of the octave—the seduction of Eve by Satan and the consequent repression of the instinctive desires of the blood—as follows:

> But old gods fall away, the ancient Snake
> Is throned and crowned instead, and has for minion
> That golden apple which will never slake
> But ever feed man's crumb of fire, when plover
> And swallow and shrill northing birds whip over
> Nazarene and Roman and Virginian.

The defeat of the old gods of the Greco-Roman mythology and the enthronement of the power of the Hebraic snake, the power of the knowledge of good and evil, paradoxically does not suppress man's cosmic "crumb of fire" but, opposing it, feeds it. Flaring up when the birds go north in the spring to nest and to renew life, it whips "over Nazarene and Roman and Virginian." That is, it wields the "whip of blood" over the dominion of Christian history. Faulkner's imagery is clumsy and its implication obvious: under the dominion of the Hebraic snake, man becomes a self-conscious sexual creature and a self-conscious historical being . . . I do not intend to say that Faulkner opposed the cosmological to the historical. I mean that his perception of history found a focus in the tension generated in the literary imagination by the conquest of the cosmic sexuality of the Greco-Roman garden by the historicism of the Hebraic-Christian interpretation of sexuality.[30]

By changing the single word "old" to "new" in *Helen* II Faulkner made a different sonnet, readily interpreted in a different way. Instead of considering "old gods" to be Greco-Roman and "new gods" to be Hebraic-Christian, this different sonnet can be thought to present the Snake as older than either; compared to the "ancient" Snake's priority in time, Greco-Roman and Hebraic-Christian are both "new." In *Helen* II Faulkner apparently thought of the serpent as it was conceived by the older mythology from which "Genesis" drew: "to be a symbol of passion and sensual pleasure."[31] Faulkner in *Helen* II seems to agree also with the view of the tree held by many Biblical scholars: "It is the serpent who says that its fruit will convey knowledge of 'good and evil'— falsely, for it brought only awareness of sex."[32] Elsewhere Faulkner appears to present a conception of the Snake in accord with this interpretation. For example, in another sonnet in *Helen*—VIII—he seems to present the effect of the Snake's involvement with Eve not as the Biblical one that Eve received knowledge of good and evil but as the popular one which has tapped the above-mentioned older symbolism of the Snake to reinterpret the Biblical account so it supports the belief that she chiefly received knowledge of sexuality: *Helen* VIII ends with the words "all the Eves unsistered since the Snake." Faulkner's term "unsistered" has puzzled many readers. Without great confidence I interpret "unsistered" to mean that before the confrontation with the Snake Eve and Adam were as sister and brother but after it Eve lost her role of sister in the new role of sexual partner. That accords with what the text of *Helen* II appears to be saying: The aspect of the Snake which concerned Faulkner when he created that version was the

Snake's fostering rather than repressing sexuality. The paradox mentioned above as being in *A Green Bough* XLII is absent from the version in *Helen* II and the imagery is less clumsy because the Snake which Faulkner presents in the *Helen* version never in past or present opposed but always fed and fanned "man's crumb of fire."

No solid conclusion may be possible about that puzzling matter, just as there may be none for another mystery—a small one about the last word of this sonnet. All known versions end with "Virginian," and one wonders why. Faulkner in the last lines drew on *A Shropshire Lad* as in these *Helen* poems and others he did often. (Too often, according to the judgment expressed in holograph marginal notes in some of the typescripts.) Faulkner's source here, as many critics have noted, is Housman's "Wenlock Edge." In that widely read poem the modern observer of a strong wind troubling the trees of the Edge is linked with the Roman of centuries before, stationed on his Empire's frontier and experiencing the same wind, which becomes in the observer's concept "the gale of life." Now the Roman and "his trouble / Are ashes" and for the modern observer too the gale of life quickly will "be gone." "Wenlock Edge" was a poem Faulkner often quoted to Meta Wilde, she told me in the second of scores of conversations about Faulkner between 1963 and the present. Later, in a letter of September 5, 1968, she wrote as follows (in this quotation, nothing has been omitted, there are no ellipses):

> About the "Wenlock Edge" . . I don't recall that Bill ever quoted the whole of it . . but two of the verses I know he did . . . The two beginning "Then, 'twas before my time" . . and the next stanza, "There, like the wind through woods in riot." Carvel, Bill seldom quoted an entire poem . . but with whatever thoughts that were crowding his mind, he seemed to pull out of memory a verse that would remind him of something at the time or make a

point. He liked to hear the sound of the words, the
rhythm of certain sounds it seemed to me . . and then
again he would be trying to help me learn through making
the philosophical thought implied clear to me.

The two stanzas Faulkner would quote, the third and fourth, explicitly link the speaker and the Roman, reducing or eliminating the barrier of time and showing that always human life is troubled. Faulkner drew from "Wenlock Edge" in several early, charred typescript versions of a poem there titled "Roland" and eventually published untitled as *A Green Bough* XXI. It presumably is drawing on Housman's "the gale of life blew high" when it says "though amain / Life's gale may blow." One of the sections about Hightower in *Light in August* is in debt to "Wenlock Edge" when it speaks of the "harsh gale of living." But Faulkner's most interesting—or at least most puzzling—use of this general material is in his holograph version of *The Sound and the Fury*.[33]

At the beginning of Quentin Compson's monologue in lines which do not appear in the published novel, Faulkner twice used the entire last line of *Helen* II: "Nazarene and Roman and Virginian." The first time, the words of that line are preceded by references to Jesus and his having no sister and are followed by the statement that they had no sister. The second time, he followed that same group of words which he had used as the last line of *Helen* II by a statement that Centurions slew some of them, then he replaced Centurions by Praetorians, and finally, striking out all those words after "Virginian," substituted in the margin a statement to the effect that none of you were crucified but were worn away by time. That the idea of crucifixion in the novel's holograph may not have been absent in *Helen* II is just possibly suggested by Faulkner's changing in line 13 the bird which is one of the birds which "whip over / Nazarene and Roman and Virginian" from the "eagle" of the burned typescript at Phil Stone's house and the "March" version now at the Berg Collection to the "swallow" of whatever other versions I have seen, the swallow being the bird which Christian tradition says flew over Jesus on the cross, a matter which Quentin Compson seems to remember in a part of the holograph when he thinks, "O sister swallow," admittedly a phrase in Swinburne's "Itylus" but in a quite different context here.

"Nazarene" is easy enough. The meaning of "Roman" because of the linkage to the "Roman" in *Helen* II, who is linked by the whipping wind to the "Roman" in "Wenlock Edge," may be easy though it probably is complicated, with the Roman representing those who crucified the Nazarene. But the "Virginian" has defied even making an interesting guess. If Faulkner in *Helen* II like Housman in "Wenlock Edge" meant, for concrete impact, to make himself the modern member of the association or in *The Sound and the Fury* holograph meant Quentin to put himself in the same role or into a role in a crucifixion, "Virginian" is not the correct word. If in both poem and novel draft Faulkner meant the "Roman" to be, as Housman did, any old Roman, he may have meant something equally general by "Virginian," though that seems unsatisfactory. The endless possibilities for speculation include George Washington and Robert E. Lee as high on the list because honor is the distraught Quentin's false and masking self-justification for his suicide, but that has little to do with the "Virginian" in *Helen* II unless Faulkner meant there that human beings of all qualities are equally subject to the "whip of blood" as birds returning north with spring pass "over / Nazarene and Roman and Virginian." Probably many already know what Faulkner had in mind here. If so, it will be good to read their conclusion.

III.

For its first appearance—in the April, 1925, issue of the

Double Dealer—this sonnet was titled "The Faun." Harold Levy, one of Faulkner's acquaintances at New Orleans, talking about the sonnet when I was preparing to reprint it in a volume of Faulkner's apprentice writings, said that during a visit with him Faulkner was having trouble writing it. After Levy helped work up part of the sonnet, Faulkner—with extreme generosity, Levy thought—credited it to Levy in an inscription on the copy of the poem Faulkner gave to him, and dedicated it "to H.L." as he was to do in the *Double Dealer* as well as one of the two typescripts of it which emerged from the burned papers at Phil Stone's house. It was reprinted by Paul Romaine in his 1932 *Salmagundi* and by James E. Wobbe of the New Orleans *Item* in a 1954 article based on information from Harold Levy. Among the Rowan Oak Papers at the University of Virginia Library is a typed version titled "The Faun" but with no dedication to "H.L." and with several changes of wording as well as a shift of the faun from March so that the first line is "When April like a faun whose stampings ring." Its last line, more negative than the last line of the version Faulkner gave to Helen Baird, is "Sip wine of old despair and brief delight."

With the exception of the typescript in the Rowan Oak Papers, lines 11 and 12 in all the known versions of the poem are: "Left bare by wild vines' slipping, does incite / To strip the musicked leaves upon her breast." These lines, like many others in Faulkner's poetry, are indebted to Swinburne, but they come from what were apparently Faulkner's favorite Swinburne lines. When Meta Wilde was recalling the poems and parts of poems by various authors which Faulkner frequently quoted to her, she identified several stanzas by Swinburne. Later, in a letter of January 17, 1964, accompanying a generous gift of the volume of Swinburne which Faulkner had bought for her in Stanley Rose's shop and from which he read to her, she helpfully said, "I have marked for you . . . those stanzas he most often quoted. He seemed to love best the lines

. . . I have marked with two small x's." The lines are in the "Chorus" of "Atalanta in Calydon" which begins "When the hounds of spring are on winter's traces" and the two x's are beside the lines at the start of the seventh stanza of that particular "Chorus":

> The ivy falls with the Bacchanal's hair
>   Over her eyebrows hiding her eyes;
> The wild vine slipping down leaves bare
>   Her bright breast shortening into sighs . . .

Faulkner drew on these lines several times, for his first published poem, as an example, and for *Helen: A Courtship* briefly in IV and V as well as here in III, and even in *Elmer*.

For *Helen* III Faulkner revised the earlier, published version and gave the sonnet greater clarity by three of his changes: Line 3 in the *Double Dealer*, "May's anticipated dryad, mute," is better in *Helen*: "Of May, anticipated dryad, mute." The beginning of line 8 is clearer because of the change from "Out-pace" to "Retrace." And certainly the whole of line 8 as it appeared in the *Double Dealer* and the typescripts, "Out-pace waned moons to May hand shapes and grieves," becomes clearer when revised in *Helen* to "Retrace waned moons to May for whom he grieves." Faulkner's revising helps make even more obvious that the power of spring is the subject of the sonnet, and faun and nymph only figures for March and May.

Less figurative fauns appeared in Faulkner's poetry from almost the beginning. Characters specifically equated to fauns also appear in his fiction, and Pan, chief of all, was especially interesting to Faulkner.

Faulkner's first published book, *The Marble Faun* (1924), has, of course, a faun at its center. According to Faulkner he wrote the basis of that volume in the spring of 1919. The next year he wrote his play, *The Marionettes*, in which the central figure is Pierrot. Noel Polk's interesting introduction to *The*

Marionettes connects those two early Faulkner protagonists through Hermes, father of Pan and inventor of the reed pipe "and the lyre, which Faulkner surely intends us to associate with Pierrot's mandolin" in the play;[34] through Mallarmé, whose faun in "L'Après-Midi d'un Faune" "dreams the same dream" as Pierrot; and through a two-page burned fragment of a poem from Phil Stone's house.[35] There may be another connection between Faulkner's faun and Pierrot: The tightest linking of the two known to Faulkner which it has been possible so far to come upon is by George Moore in his *Memoirs of My Dead Life* (1906). That volume seems never to have been studied in relation to Faulkner, but one of his college friends told me in 1950 that Faulkner in 1919 had been extremely fond of it. Moore in his *Memoirs* mentions fauns a number of times, but his linking Pierrot to them is in this passage:

> Pierrot, the white, sensual animal, the eighteenth-century modification of the satyr, of the faun, plays a guitar; the pipe of Pan has been exchanged for a guitar.[36]

This sonnet and the following one, the only poems in the tradition of satyrs, fauns, dryads, and nymphs which Faulkner permitted himself in *Helen*, bring up another related subject in Faulkner's writing, one for which he also probably owed something to Moore's *Memoirs*. Nympholepsy concerned Faulkner in several of his works and in recent years has been discussed often in print since the Henry W. and Albert A. Berg Collection at the New York Public Library acquired Faulkner's unpublished essay "Nympholepsy" among the papers Faulkner had left at New Orleans in 1925.

Reading files of the University of Mississippi student newspaper at the end of the 1940's and finding that Faulkner had published enough writings there in 1919 and the few following years to warrant republishing them as a volume, it was especially pleasant to find an unsigned, well-written prose sketch titled "The Hill" which seemed to be by him and interestingly related to several of his other works. It was additionally pleasant to find in the next week's issue the editor's apology for having omitted from the sketch the author's initials, W.F.[37] Years later hearing that the Berg Collection perhaps had bought several Faulkner typescripts, and writing to ask whether that was true, it was good to receive an immediate affirmative reply from the Collection's effective Curator, Dr. Lola Szladits, saying there was no public announcement as yet but she was glad for the chance to share the news and that the documents were available for study. Among them was the typescript of "Nympholepsy," an interesting, though less well executed, outgrowth of "The Hill." The protagonist of "The Hill"—a laborer at the end of the day's work looking down on a town and thinking dimly but movingly about life—or a man much like him reappears in "Nympholepsy." In an expansion of a somewhat chilly reference to nymphs and fauns in "The Hill," the protagonist of "Nympholepsy" at the end of the day sees or thinks he sees a girl in the woods and follows her. She fleetly eludes him, but during the chase he falls into a stream and, in a motif which appears elsewhere in Faulkner's works, believes she too is in the water and associates her there with death.

Since "Nympholepsy" was published in 1973[38] there have been various nominations in print of possible literary sources for Faulkner's concept and for his essay's title. I submit that Moore's *Memoirs* probably was influential. Two years after Faulkner's friend said Faulkner was extremely interested in the *Memoirs*, another of his friends said Faulkner was especially attracted to the book's once famous—in fact, notorious—long section, "The Lovers of Orelay."

In that section, which Moore presented as autobiography but experts on his voluminous works think was probably an imaginative expansion of one of his early poems, Moore says to his companion, Doris:

> "You ask me why I like the landscape? Because it carries me back into past times when men believed in nymphs

and in satyrs. I have always thought it must be a wonderful thing to believe in the dryad. Do you know that men wandering in the woods sometimes used to catch sight of a white breast between the leaves, and henceforth they could love no mortal woman. The beautiful name of their malady was nympholepsy. A disease that every one would like to catch."[39]

Moore's definition relates to part of Faulkner's "Nympholepsy"—though, as mentioned above, Faulkner's sketch emphasizes a harsher element, the nearness of death—and to similar affecting sightings in some of Faulkner's other works, an extremely minor and incomplete though focused example being the first line of the other sonnet in *Helen* which uses fauns and nymphs, IV.[40]

Moore's *Memoirs of My Dead Life*, which has a long section about the Luxembourg Gardens, appears in the Elmer papers, when Faulkner speaks of the Luxembourg as "that homely informal garden where the ghost of George Moore's dead life wanders politely in a pale eroticism . . ." Also in 1925, in his newspaper essay on Sherwood Anderson, Faulkner said that "George Moore is interesting only when he is telling about the women he has loved or the clever things he has said."[41] Despite this somewhat disenchanted view, the book may have influenced Faulkner through his early, admiring reading of it in other small ways beyond whatever he may have taken about fauns, Pierrot, and nympholepsy. Moore at length discusses Verlaine, some of whose poems Faulkner early translated or, rather, rewrote. Moore calls him "The singer of the sweetest verses in the French language," "the only poet that Catholicism has produced since Dante,"[42] a poet weaned "away from ideas—the curse of modern literature" so that he is "a sort of divine vagrant."[43] One can speculate—only—that Faulkner's beginning to speak of figures from Tanagra may owe something to Moore, for it is a reference Moore makes at least five times in describing Doris in "The Lovers of Orelay."[44] Faulkner's reactions to the Luxembourg Gardens seem to reflect Moore's in his *Memoirs*.

Though George Moore's great concern that the setting for love-making be romantic was not required to turn Faulkner to that view, it presumably was supportive of Faulkner's personal inclination. Moore and Doris in "The Lovers of Orelay," having found the perfect hotel suite, unsuccessfully search the shops of the entire town to buy Moore silk pajamas for their first night of love. Though that quest is naive and unintentionally funny, Moore's well expressed romantic feelings for setting came to mind during one of the many drives around Los Angeles with Meta Wilde who generously offered to visit places she had been with Faulkner so she could discuss the recollections invoked by her seeing them again: Passing the Miramar Hotel at Santa Monica in December, 1963, she recalled that the first time she and Faulkner stayed there he surprised and pleased her by spreading over the bed a blanket of gardenias which she said he called jasmine and had made for them without telling her, an action which she wrote of a dozen years later in her book with Orin Borsten, *A Loving Gentleman: The Love Story of William Faulkner and Meta Carpenter*.[45] For that pleasant act no ardent, imaginative, romantic lover needs a literary source (though the idea could have been augmented for Faulkner by *The Temptation of St. Anthony*, Elinor Glyn's *Three Weeks*, and other books he had read written by the non-allergic), but Faulkner's attitude was certainly in accord with that of the author of those *Memoirs* which his friends reported had interested him inordinately in his early twenties. In his late forties, when Henriette Martin, who was a good friend of Meta's, asked whether he was a mystic, he vehemently denied it, she told me, but when she went on to say to him that he was a romantic, Faulkner replied that *that* he certainly was. In his mid-fifties he wrote down thoughts of covering a bed with violets.

In Moore's *Memoirs of My Dead Life* are other elements which might be tied to Faulkner but to mention only a small single possibility perhaps pertinent here: Invited to sail on Lake Sardis in Faulkner's little sloop, the *Ring Dove*, it was interesting, having recently read Moore's *Memoirs*, to hear Mrs. Faulkner's explanation that the boat was named for one in Conrad's "The End of the Tether" and to realize that Faulkner expressed no disagreement. The *Ringdove* in Conrad is a fast commercial sailing vessel mentioned two or three times as having been captained by one of the protagonist's friends years before. Moore's "The Lovers of Orelay," of which Faulkner was reported to have been so especially fond, mentions briefly a different *Ring-Dove*, a sailing yacht with romantic connotations for Moore, and his readers. On that *Ring-Dove*, chartered by a charming, wealthy lover, Moore and she had once planned to cruise for a season in the Greek Islands (which were attractive enough to Faulkner for him inaccurately to report, many years later, that he had visited them in 1925). If one source of his sloop's name actually was Moore's "Lovers of Orelay," Faulkner may have decided that, as with innumerable more important aspects of his life, this romantic private detail was just that: private, entirely. A legitimate smoke screen of diversionary misstatement, like that which fills his published interviews and question-and-answer sessions, may have been operating. Later, in 1955, he told a newspaper reporter the boat was named "after a famous racing clipper."[46]

Because of Faulkner's early and continuing extreme concern about mortality and escaping annihilation he probably noted the thoughts Moore expressed when ending *Memoirs of My Dead Life*: Moore's mind reached for "the unattainable, seeking that which Rameses had been unable to find" and concluded somewhat optimistically that the whole cycle of the development of the universe will be repeated. "It is like madness, but is it madder than Christian doctrine? and I believe that billions of years hence, billions and billions of years hence, I shall be sitting in the same room where I sit now, writing the same lines I am now writing . . ."[47] Faulkner with intensity tried throughout his life many ways to deal with annihilation, and here Moore early offered one of them, which Faulkner later discussed, though he seemed to find it unsatisfactory.

So Moore may have affected Faulkner by offering him a little more than just the statement first cited by Phil Stone in 1924, often repeated since, and best described by John McClure as "George Moore's penetrating half-truth that literature to be universal must first be provincial."[48]

Memoirs of My Dead Life illustrates part of the problem biographers and critics have in determining what books Faulkner read and what he thought of them. The *Catalogue* of the books which were in Faulkner's possession at his death, published in 1964,[49] is very helpful, but students of Faulkner often misuse it when they forget its admonition that the presence of a book on the list does not mean Faulkner read it—people mailed him many unsolicited and not always appealing volumes, for example—nor does the absence of a book, such as *Memoirs of My Dead Life*, mean that Faulkner did not read it—he borrowed books from innumerable willing lenders, read books at hosts' houses, and must have left purchased books behind him in many places, judging from his doing so at New Orleans and Paris. Meta Wilde and A. I. Bezzarides both told me that they observed Faulkner's buying of an enormous number of books, at much too fast a rate for his library at his death to be no larger than it was.

Problems with what he thought of the books he owned also exist because the "Introduction" to that catalogue of Faulkner's library contains a widely believed statement that the "one reliable sign" of Faulkner's "esteem" for the books he owned is that he wrote his name and customarily a place and a date in those "he cared about."[50] A large portion of the studies of Faulkner written since the appearance of that "Introduction" base some argument on that statement, concluding that a book did or did not influence Faulkner's fiction because he did or did not like the book as indicated by whether or not he wrote his name in it.

Examination of the *Catalogue*'s list of Faulkner's books shows such a conclusion, improbable enough on the face of it, to be unsupportable. To take only one example, Faulkner wrote his name, the name of his Oxford house, and a 1938 date in each of the four volumes of *The Public Papers and Addresses of Franklin D. Roosevelt* now at his Rowan Oak library. Random House, which published it, had sent to him as a gift the five-volume set, from which the second volume later disappeared. Faulkner intensely disliked the presidency of Franklin Roosevelt and without question did not care for or hold in esteem Roosevelt's political papers and addresses, but he inscribed those volumes.

More dramatic evidence that Faulkner's inscribing his name, a place, and a date in one of his books does not prove he had esteem for it is supplied by a book not in Faulkner's possession at his death: the copy of Flaubert's *The Temptation of St. Anthony* which was mentioned above. In 1925 Faulkner owned in France, and left there when he came home, a paperback copy, in French. The book turned up years later for sale at a Seine book stall. In it Faulkner had written his name, a place, and a 1925 date. But instead of having esteem for the book Faulkner wrote in it an angry attack, accusing it of shaming *Madame Bovary*. He ended his paragraph of vituperation by thanking God that Flaubert had died. Certainly an extreme of emotion in hostile literary criticism, very far beyond even that of Faulknerian cabals. Nevertheless Faulkner inscribed in the book his name, a place, and a date. Faulkner's low initial opinion of the book agreed with that of Flaubert's intimate literary friends, who had urged him to destroy the manuscript. Perhaps Faulkner's early opinion of the book was low chiefly because he read it in French that first time, when he may still have had some difficulty with the language. Years later he reversed his opinion in the well-known interviews of 1955 with Cynthia Grenier and 1956 with Jean Stein, ranking *The Temptation* with the Old Testament and Marlowe's plays, works which it made him "feel good" to read.[51] But for him earlier to inscribe his copy of *The Temptation* with his name, a place, and a date yet write in it also that violently hostile commentary—one of the extremely few commentaries, favorable or unfavorable, he ever inscribed in a book—belies the biographical conception which has become so widely accepted.

That misconception about there being significance in the presence or absence of Faulkner's autograph in books he owned has become so established it will survive as long as Faulkner is studied; so we can imagine one outcome: the second volume of Faulkner's gift set of Roosevelt's *Public Papers*, in which he wrote his name, a place, and a date as he did in the other four volumes, is missing from his library because one of Faulkner's acquaintances, I have been told, sent it to a friend interested in both Faulkner and Roosevelt who would in exchange send back for Faulkner's library the uninscribed second volume from his own set. Like the conclusion of many plans, this one apparently has not yet happened. But if it does, we can anticipate someday reading a book about Faulkner's involvement in politics which—because its problem of finding something to say could approach that of the fabled book on snakes in Ireland—will report with relief, accompanied by detailed analysis, that Faulkner liked Roosevelt's political beliefs in Volumes I, III, IV, and V but obviously hated those in Volume II.

IV

Faulkner later published this sonnet without a title as XLI

in *A Green Bough*. Some surviving typescripts of it have the title "Old Satyr." A charred typescript at Phil Stone's house bore a holograph date in 1924. So here again Faulkner in assembling *Helen: A Courtship* was updating a poem to the three weeks in June, 1925, during which he spent some time with Helen Baird at Pascagoula in the intervals of steadfast work finishing his first novel.

Actually Faulkner was updating the writing of the sonnet at least one year more than that, for he almost certainly wrote it earlier than 1924: Elsewhere in the debris of the Stones' fire a typescript of this sonnet turned up in a sheaf of several poems with a cover page on which was typed, twice, "1923." Later, I believe, that dating of those poems was lost by their being separated into different categories for library filing. The next sonnet here in *Helen: A Courtship* also was in that "1923" sheaf, which is surprising.

V. "Proposal"

One critical study quite understandably assumes Faulkner imagined himself preparing to confront Helen Baird's mother when he wrote this sonnet because it so aptly fits his situation in 1925 while assembling *Helen: A Courtship*, but it appeared, like *Helen* IV, in the sheaf of "1923" poems which was partly salvageable at the site of the Stones' fire.

In a letter from Oxford to a friend in 1924 Faulkner reported that The Four Seas Company had agreed to publish *The Marble Faun* after Knopf had refused it, that he had written it in the spring of 1919 and had been trying extremely hard ever since to get it published, but that he did not like it and had a volume of much better poetry which he had held back in favor of *The Marble Faun*. Quite possibly the sheaf marked "1923" contained poems of that volume; of the sheaf's thirteen poems which were not too burned to be identified all but one were published a decade later in *A Green Bough* (1933).[52]

Here in *Helen* the sonnet is dated from Pascagoula in June of 1925, with the title "Proposal"; in the sheaf of "1923" Faulkner had titled it "In Spring a Young Man's Fancy-----." Another burned typescript—which by a change in line 8 from typed "Womb" to holograph "Find" seems to be early but by a change in line 2 from typed "grave" to holograph "smooth" seems to be quite late when compared to other versions—is dated on Faulkner's freighter voyage to Europe.

The sonnet is the first of the *Helen* cycle directly to confront, if not Helen's mother, the poet's sexual desire for his beloved. In the sexuality of preceding *Helen* sonnets, Faulkner had involved only Eve, a dryad, a nymph, several fauns, and a satyr. While expressing the poet's own desire here he may have been a little too coy in wording line 7, but he was direct enough. And he gave the sonnet quality by the humor of interrupting the poet's preparation of his speech to a mother by his erotic thoughts about her daughter.

Recently much has been written concerning Faulkner's sexuality, and too much of it seems off the mark. That might be illustrated by taking just two samples from the most recent biography, which apparently developed theories first and then conformed the evidence to support them. This practice has been common enough in the criticism of Faulkner's fiction, where, to mention only one example, a writer who wants Faulkner to have been a life-long optimistic humanist must distort tragic early novels by arguing that they have happy endings. Now it apparently is biography's turn.

The first sample concerns some drawings Faulkner gave in 1936 to Meta Wilde, which she describes on page 75 of *A Loving Gentleman*. Her description shows clearly that the drawings are not, as the biography surprisingly concludes, "apparently so highly stylized as to resemble inspired outlines of lovers."[53] For the biography to misinterpret her description of the drawings in that inaccurate way supports its view of Faulkner's sexuality, but certainly the drawings themselves do not support it. When Meta Wilde let me photocopy them along with her other Faulkner documents it seemed well not to risk losing the copies on the remainder of an extended trip but to mail them directly home. Because of the active role of the Post Office in censorship at that time—the editor of *Eros* was in prison for sending his magazine through the mails— the package was wrapped with extreme care. When I finally reached Cambridge the local Postmaster called me to his office and showed me the package, the extraordinary wrapping of which had been no more deterrent than rain, sleet, and gloom of night. The Postmaster said that when the contents of the broken package had been shown to his superiors they considered taking action. But he went on to say that after he pointed out the nature of the investigation I was trying to make, and that mailing the package from myself to myself hardly constituted distribution, they dropped the matter. Even the Post Office of that day would not have been upset by the drawings if they were what the biography chooses to speculate they are, contrary to what Meta wrote about them in her book.

The twenty-six drawings are explicit and show Faulkner to be imaginative in many ways. The accomplished novelist, Monique Lange, whom I had interviewed some years before, told me, while she was giving a filmed interview at her Paris apartment for the recent television documentary on Faulkner, that she might be accepting an invitation to write one volume for a famous series. She perceptively said the goal should be to make the novel "erotic but not pornographic." Faulkner achieved that in these drawings—which are not "highly stylized . . . inspired outlines"—by doing them seriously, explicitly, and intensely but with humor, somewhat as he used humor in this *Helen* sonnet of sexual desire and in the conclusion of *Light in August* when the furniture dealer and his wife by their humor while in bed together make a sane, free contrast to the sexual confusion in the rest of the novel. The basic concept of Faulkner's drawings was witty: Working at a film studio, Faulkner on a slack day, thinking of Meta while being paid to be there to make films, made drawings which suggest they are animation stills and would give the illusion of movement if seen in rapid sequence. As he was supposed to do in that office, he made a movie. Man in motion. His humorous perspective continued in the line he used for the drawings and in the detumescence of the final picture, which Meta describes in *A Loving Gentleman*. Faulkner strengthened his suggestion that the drawings are a sequence of animation stills when he wrote at their conclusion all but the last word of the brief sentence with which a long-running series ends each of its animated cartoons: "That's all folks."

The other sample illustration selected from the same biography also bears on this sonnet, *Helen* V, because of Faulkner's use of "moons" in lines 4 and 5. The biography quotes—and seriously misinterprets in the interest of a theory about Faulkner's sexuality—the last five lines of this eight-line Faulkner poem which Meta Wilde records in her book:

> Red thy famble,
> White thy gan,
> And thy quaranon.
> Dainty is couth
> Couch thy moons.
> Mid with me then
> In the darkness
> Clip and kiss.[54]

Another—written—version of the poem which Faulkner presented to Meta is:

> Red thy fambles, white thy gan,
> And thy quarrons dainty is.
> Couch thy moons' mid with me then.
> In the darkmans clip and kiss.

To foster a theory, the biography elects to interpret this poem, with its "moons," as an effort by Faulkner, in his "fear of being contaminated," to move "his lover back" to "a time before the onset" of menstruation. To support this unsupportable reading of the poem, the biography quotes Quentin Compson's disastrous father's misogynist statement associating "moons" (astronomical) with what the character calls women's "periodical filth," and cites as well the confusions of unfortunate Joe Christmas on the subject.[55]

In both of the poem's versions the poet, clearly, is praising the body of a woman and asking her to go to bed with him to make love. The "moons" he invites her to "couch" are not astronomical and related to menstruation but anatomical and obviously the hips or thighs. That Faulkner meant the "moons" in line 4 of this sonnet, *Helen* V, to be in apposition with "hips" is made clear by line 5. If further proof were needed one could cite lines 3 and 4 of a typed version which is in the Rowan Oak Papers at the University of Virginia: "And momently the cloyed and clotted bees / Where hive her honeyed thighs, those little moons." In that version Faulkner first typed "hips" then canceled it on the typewriter and immediately after it typed "thighs." *Helen* V and the poem for Meta praise the beloved's body and make proposals. So does Faulkner's source for the poem to Meta, the second stanza in a seventeenth-century song of a rogue admiringly using thieves' cant to describe his lover's body and ask her to go to bed with him. As Richard Head published it in the fourth canting song of *The Canting Academy*, London, 1673, page 19, the stanza is:

> White thy fambles, red thy gan,
> And thy quarrons dainty is,
> Couch a hogshead with me than,
> In the Darkmans clip and kiss.

The general vocabulary in Head's volume gives these meanings for the cant words of that stanza: "fambles," hands; "gans," lips; "quarron," body; "couch a hogshead," to go to sleep; "darkmans," night or evening. Faulkner's variations from the stanza in Head, including the reversal of colors for "fambles" and "gan," are not surprising; he understandably sometimes remembered poems inexactly, other examples being various transcriptions of one of his favorites, Joyce's "Watching the Needleboats at San Sabba." Among them are one he sent to Helen Baird Lyman in a letter from California and one he wrote in a book for Anthony Buttitta, now in Carl Petersen's excellent Faulkner collection.

Before leaving the subject of moons, a note about the apparently erroneous apostrophe in this sonnet's fifth line: "These slender moons' unsunder I would break." The first editorial reaction would be to remove the apostrophe on the assumption that by "unsunder" Faulkner really meant "asunder." But on reflection, he seems to have meant "unsunder" to be an attribute of the moons, a condition of, say, togetherness. Whether we need that difficulty is questionable, but the presence of the apostrophe is not.

VI

Opening with an answer to a question which the mother asked in the last line of the preceding sonnet and continuing to show that thoughts of the girl he loves intrude on thoughts about talking with her mother, the poet is no longer explicit concerning the longed-for act of love but is admiring of his beloved's body, her movements, her sensual presence. Though it obviously forms a pair with *Helen* V, it was not among the legible poems in the charred sheaf of "1923" and has not turned up so far in any holograph or typewritten versions. So probably, with *Helen* V on hand, Faulkner did write this one in 1925 to make the pair. Some support for such a guess may come from the fact that the concept of "Twin timorous" rabbits in line 10 is repeated by a statement Faulkner assigned in *Mosquitoes* to Dawson Fairchild, for whose character

Faulkner drew on his association with Sherwood Anderson in 1925.

While continuing to think biographically about *Helen* rather than critically and having mentioned Faulkner's sexuality in discussing the first of this pair of sonnets, it seems well to add here that Meta Wilde has made the excellent point that Faulkner was not "a womanizer."[56] Acquaintances of Faulkner, in Oxford, other Mississippi towns, Memphis, New Haven, Toronto, New York, New Orleans, Hollywood, Las Vegas, Taxco, Tokyo, and Paris have agreed, by volunteering that Faulkner was not, as several of them phrased it, "a chaser."

Some biographical study has been rather harshly judgmental about what it assumes was Faulkner's patronage of professional prostitutes in early years when he said, jokingly, that he was off to Memphis to do research for his novels. But according to the comments of several people who had opportunities to know, he seems not to have employed prostitutes at all. The madam of a busy brothel which he often visited volunteered more than once in the several times I called on her, to do research, that Faulkner never hired the services of her employees, that he came to her place for the liquor she sold in those Prohibition times, for talk with her as a good friend saying he wanted to put some of her life into a novel (which he did), and for a brief change from Oxford in the company of friends. In his fifties Faulkner made a statement parallel in formula to Wilbourne's famous declaration after Charlotte's death in *The Wild Palms*: Faulkner wrote (paraphrased, genteelly, here) that between loving without copulating and copulating without loving he would take the former.

Some of his friends have said in interviews over several years that when Faulkner fell in love he did so very romantically and valued his involvement with the whole being of the woman he loved.

VII

In a burned typescript version of this sonnet Faulkner made a number of holograph revisions. His changes in the last three lines included some reversal in details of the meaning. He originally ended the typescript:

> .... sweep
> A beauty calm and passionless; forgets
> Tomorrow is what yesterday begets,
> That husbandless or not, gains doubtful sleep.

He then revised the three lines by pen:

> .... sweep
> A beauty true and passionate, but forgets
> That flowers but must die, and that regrets
> Buy only one thing sure: undoubtful sleep.

He later revised further for the final version here in *Helen* VII:

> .... sweep
> A beauty fixed and true, but she forgets
> The dream once touched must fade, and that regrets
> Buy only one thing sure: undoubtful sleep.

That final wording at the start of the next to last line, "The dream once touched must fade," seems to echo the Cabellian theme of Faulkner's other gift to Helen Baird, *Mayday*. (It also seems not the best choice of argument for a poet trying to persuade his reluctant beloved to capitulate.)

One pleasant improvement of tone in a poem attempting some mythological grandeur was the change in line 9 to "Hail," from the typescript's rather flat "Hello." That Faulkner retained in all the versions I have seen the obsolete spelling of "skull" for "scull" seems in keeping.

The sonnet obviously shares much with Faulkner's longer poem "Hymn," a typescript of which Faulkner's grandaunt

'Bama McLean owned and in 1951 generously allowed me to photocopy along with the rest of her documents relating to Faulkner. Another, variant, typescript version of "Hymn" was in the Stone fire. Even more vigorous than *Helen* VII, "Hymn" shares with it the linkage of centaur and beauty. The first of its four stanzas, in the version at the Stone house, is this:

> Where shall we seek thee, O beauty? Aloft in the morning
> Where the hooves of the centaur ring like brass on the hill,
> Gold as flame where the flame of the young year runs
> Through leaf and copse, swelling as music swells?
> Glittering leaves are shaken and soundless bells
> To the centaur's rush: his hooves are a myriad suns
> In the strength of his fire to love, in the fire of his strength to kill.
> Where shall we seek thee, O beauty, if not in the morning?

"Hymn," and through it *Helen* VII, is in debt to a section of Swinburne's poetry which Meta Wilde kindly marked for me in her volume of Swinburne as one from which Faulkner often quoted to her: the "Chief Huntsman's Song" in "Atalanta in Calydon." From one of its choruses, the one mentioned earlier which begins "When the hounds of spring are on winter's traces," "Hymn" drew on such elements as "Where shall we find her," "fire," "wind," and the exuberance of springtime. In that uplifted spirit Faulkner's "Hymn" even repudiates "death" and "derision" which are mentioned in Swinburne's more somber next chorus; line 24 of "Hymn" says that "gone" are "All who have Death for father, Derision for mother." This linkage of death and derision also occurs elsewhere in Faulkner's work, in the poem "Twilight" (*A Green Bough* X), which is related to Faulkner's sketches, "The Hill" and "Nympholepsy," and in "Nympholepsy" itself—all apparently partially indebted to this section of Swinburne which Faulkner years afterward still took pleasure in quoting often.

The final stanza of "Hymn" moves, like the sestina of this sonnet, toward the somber:

> Where shall we seek thee? Between the sunrise and dawning,
> Between sleep, the sister of death; and death, the brother of sleep?

Then, though in awareness of the power of death, it ends uplifted in the spring woods:

> > Where glittering limbs in dance make light
> > Like doves in silver-feathered flight.
> Let us but find thee, though we lose life in thy sweep.
> Where shall we seek thee, O beauty, if not in the morning?

Differing in tone from that, the ending of *Helen* VII is fully somber, but the change serves the poet's need in this sonnet cycle to persuade his beloved to delay no more.

The charred typescript of *Helen* VII is titled "Helen and the Centaur" and now seems likely to have been written with Helen Baird in mind. A first assumption naturally might be that the Helen in the sonnet probably came like the Centaur out of classic myth, that she was Helen of the Trojan War, the paragon of feminine attractiveness whom Faulkner sometimes brought into his fiction. But joined with the burned typescript titled "Helen and the Centaur" was a typescript version of the next sonnet, *Helen* VIII, "Virginity," with the title "Helen and Virginity." Because virginity was not an issue with Helen of Troy but is central to this sonnet cycle, "Helen and Virginity" presumably was titled with Helen Baird in mind. So she may also be the Helen of this sonnet, for the two typescripts are paired not only by their typescript titles and their location within the debris from the Stone fire, but by being the only sonnets in the *Helen* cycle attempting to persuade the woman not to delay her decision to make love with the poet.

VIII "Virginity"

At the end of this first of the cycle's sonnets to be dated after he left Pascagoula, Faulkner suggested he wrote it on Majorca. The surviving official papers of the freighter on which he was a passenger do not show any stop there, and Faulkner probably more accurately placed the writing of a now charred typescript of this sonnet "at sea, S S West Ivis." For him to want to put "MAJORCA" rather than "at sea" into the lettering of his romantic sonnet cycle for Helen Baird is easy to understand.

The charred typescript showed a title, "Helen and Virginity," badly scorched but complete when I first dried it out on the Stones' lawn; later its beginning fell away. To some published versions, all fundamentally the same in spite of small variations, Faulkner gave another title: "To a Virgin." The sonnet also appeared, untitled, as *A Green Bough* XXXIX.

The content and intent of the poem until near its end are fairly simple *carpe diem* as mentioned above, but in its final few lines, even if "unsistered since the Snake" means what was conjectured above in the section about *Helen* II, the poem becomes quite difficult. There is even more difficulty in the next sonnet.

IX

Faulkner dated what seems to me his most impenetrable sonnet from Genoa, where he and Spratling left the *West Ivis* on August 2, 1925, twenty-seven days out of New Orleans. No other versions of it are known to exist.

Faulkner never published it, and one wonders whether

there is any chance that was because he felt it would be incomprehensible to many readers. "Difficult" is a term often applied to Faulkner's fiction, and much of the best of it is far from easy. But one can argue that in his fiction the difficulty is not gratuitous, is profitable to the perceptive and interested reader. True, in a few nodes of extreme difficulty such as the cryptic account of Jason Compson's cotton speculation or the poker scene of "Was" in *Go Down, Moses*, a particular turn of Faulkner's mind, sometimes also demonstrated outside his poetry and fiction, made him indulge himself in playing an intricate game, and though readers usually can work out the details to make sense, sometimes esthetically very significant sense, they can do so only by withdrawing temporarily from the forward motion of the novel. But those nodes of detailed difficulty are rare in his fiction, and the difficulties of the rest of the fiction are usually a major part of what makes the novels attractive. If *Absalom, Absalom!*, for example, were really primarily about Sutpen's plantation-building experience and the novel were told in the easy chronological order which would best serve such a purpose, we would be paying no more attention to *Absalom, Absalom!* today than we are to T. S. Stribling's decently done trilogy. The involute structure of *Absalom, Absalom!* is difficult but profitable in its effective contribution to what the novel is about; and its difficulty, contrary to being gratuitous, is essential and rewarding. Conrad Aiken put it well shortly before Faulkner received the Nobel Prize: Telling a newspaper reporter that Faulkner "is the great American genius, the only adult writer of fiction we've had in the last twenty years on a major scale," he went on to say that Faulkner's intricacy, "the so-called rococo in Faulkner, even when it becomes almost intolerable, is valuable as a part of that complexity of form, that density" which "texture must have."[57]

I believe one could support an argument that often in Faulkner's poetry, for example in the final lines of the previous sonnet and all of this one, there is unprofitable difficulty but that when he changed his creative emphasis from poetry to fiction he found that the willingness and ability to be difficult which had damaged his poetry could, in the less intense medium of fiction, be extremely effective. This may have been one of the major profits which his fiction received from his apprenticeship to poetry.

Shakespere's *Sonnets* were solidly in Faulkner's mind. He quoted a few of them often. Aware that they include some of the most difficult writing in English, he was also aware that their difficulties which yield only grudgingly to the intellect often make deep emotional effect. There is a rumor that after a number of sophisticates had almost agreed in a Hollywood discussion that any literary work which the intellect could not readily comprehend was defective, Faulkner merely quoted into a silence Shakespeare's Sonnet 129, which ended the discussion. At another social gathering, Robert N. Linscott wrote, "a guest was indicting modern poetry on the ground that all good poetry must be clear and simple. When he paused for breath, Bill quietly recited Shakespeare's *The Phoenix and the Turtle*."[58] Unfortunately it is doubtful he could have made the point by quoting his own sonnet, *Helen* IX.[59]

It is barely possible that the difficulty which Shakespeare could bring off in his poetry was part of what led Faulkner to the mistaken employment of it in his own, for example here in *Helen* IX: *The Phoenix and the Turtle*, a difficult poem Faulkner often quoted throughout his adult life, shows Shakespeare interestingly manipulating complex paradoxes of singleness and duality: "love in twain," "Two distincts, division none," "the self was not the same; / Single nature's double name / Neither two nor one was call'd," "either neither," "twain . . . concordant one," but the two birds were together and Shakespeare was a great poet. In *Helen* IX the two basic entities are apart, which is harder, and Faulkner was not a great poet.

One can loosely speculate that if Faulkner needed literary guides to make his poetry gratuitously difficult and his fiction difficult but not gratuitously so, he may also have learned from a statement by Anatole France in *The Garden of Epicurus*, a book he admired enough to send his copy in the early nineteen-twenties to his grandaunt, Mrs. McLean: ". . . humanity is hardly ever passionately attracted by works of art or poetry which are not in some part or degree obscure and capable of various interpretations."[60]

X

No typescripts of this—comfortably comprehensible—sonnet exist, and Faulkner is not known ever to have published it. He seems rather to have quarried from it for other poems. He used the idea of its final two lines for the beginning of a poem which Meta Wilde said he often quoted when he was happy, *A Green Bough* XXIV:

> How canst thou be chaste, when lonely nights
> And nights I lay beside in intimate loveliness
> Thy grave beauty . . . .

Though it is fair to note that she said he more frequently quoted the poem's final lines:

> . . . . Then flowed
> Beneath my hand thy body's curve, and turned
> To me within the famished lonely dark
> Thy sleeping kiss.

He also drew—more—from this sonnet for another poem in *A Green Bough*, the sonnet XL, a slightly different typescript version of which is in the Rowan Oak Papers at the University of Virginia, titled "She Lies Sleeping." The poem's content in general is close to that of *Helen* X, and addressing an "oft-cozened maid, who'd not be twain" the poet repeats the idea from the conclusion of *Helen* X by saying, "Thou chaste? Why, I've lain lonely nights that fled . . ."

XI

The final five sonnets, the last third of the cycle, in one way or another bring up the subject of death, with progressively increased emphasis. This sonnet says the value which the poet gives to his Helen is so high that after death he would not want to wake in eternity even among "deathless golden Helens" of myth while he still remembered his earthly love.

Like the preceding sonnet, this one is not known in any other version. Faulkner dated both from Pavia, in an area of Italy where he stayed for a few days on the way from Genoa through Switzerland to Paris.

XII

Faulkner dated this sonnet and the next from Lago Maggiore, above which he stayed very briefly in a hill village, where he did some writing, according to his report later from Paris in a letter to Mrs. McLean which Robert Daniel kindly made available to me some years ago, in time for a look at the village while it still surprisingly retained the peace which Faulkner told Mrs. McLean he had found attractive.[61] The few days he had spent so pleasantly at the village stretched into a summer when he recalled them years later in a letter to Joan Williams from Stresa, May 12, 1953.

In this sonnet are a few of the good, terse, effectively "difficult" lines which Faulkner produced in several of the *Helen* sonnets as he moved toward ending his serious intention of giving his writing life to poetry.

XIII

Faulkner wrote holograph drafts of this poem before he sailed for Europe from New Orleans. They were among the papers he left there, almost all of which eventually went to the Berg Collection. The rare book and manuscript dealer, Robert Wilson, retained one holograph draft manuscript of this poem. It is titled "Leaving Her" and obviously is a very early stage in the sonnet's composition, the word "geese" in the second line having been canceled and replaced by the word "hawks" which remains in other versions.[62]

A later-stage holograph manuscript of the poem, also titled "Leaving Her" and also from the same group of documents Faulkner jettisoned in New Orleans, is in the McKeldin Library of the University of Maryland, where the Curator, Dr. Robert L. Beare, helpfully has pointed out that under the hand-written draft are traces of the start of a typed version.

Though this sonnet is perhaps among Faulkner's best he is not known to have published it, preferring to use part of its central concept in *A Green Bough* XXV, where lines 13–16 are:

> O I have seen
> The ultimate hawk unprop the ultimate skies,
> And with the curving image of his fall
> Locked beak to beak . . .

That is one element in a small cluster of images which appeared in his poetry and continued to be important to Faulkner the rest of his life, during which he grouped them around his feeling for love, and sometimes for the poignancy of love's passing. The elements include: Cnydos (Cnidus), the promentory city associated with Aphrodite, goddess of love and beauty, which owned one of the most celebrated of Greek statues, the Aphrodite by Praxiteles. Hawk (or eagle). The wind, sometimes "sweeping the april to lesbos / whitening the seas." The human heart, loving but sometimes troubled in awareness that all is transient.[63] In Faulkner's poetry these elements are scattered among this sonnet XIII in *Helen*, *A Green Bough* XVII, and *A Green Bough* XVII, "o atthis." Critics have understandably assumed that Faulkner wrote the last, *A Green Bough* XVII, in 1925 after he reached Paris, for he titled some versions "On Seeing the Winged Victory for the First Time." But a holograph version of it, differing somewhat from the text of *A Green Bough* XVII, was one of the poems in a charred booklet, *The Lilacs*, which turned up in the debris at the Stones' house, dated 1920.[64] A character in *Soldiers' Pay*, written before Faulkner left for Europe, quotes part of it.

The treatment here in *Helen* XIII of one element of that highly personal and persistent cluster of images and feelings is admirably adapted to the sonnet's function in the cycle, to be a transition to or introduction of the poet's full acceptance that he will never have his beloved. Using the tradition that hawks make love in an ecstatic diving fall locked beak to beak, Faulkner is effectively ironic in the sonnet's sestet when the abandoned poet-hawk, diving, "Locks beak to beak his shadowed keen distress."

XIV

Faulkner used the sestet of this sonnet as the whole of poem XXIII in *A Green Bough*. By omitting the first eight lines of the sonnet, and in the last six changing tense and omitting the reference to youth, he eliminated the sonnet's element of death from the version in *A Green Bough*. When he quoted the final line to Meta Wilde, which she said he did frequently, he presumably had in mind not this sonnet but the poem in *A Green Bough*, because in that context the reason to think "that's not for you" was his marriage (and then hers) rather than death, which dominates the Housman-like sonnet.

Death was, of course, a staple of the poetic traditions within which he wrote his poems. And the linking of love and death had not awaited publication by Freud; Thomas Pynchon makes a character in *Gravity's Rainbow* identify "the single melody, banal and exasperating, of all Romanticism since the Middle Ages: 'the act of love and the act of death are one.'"[65] But without question Faulkner, going far beyond literary models, was inordinately concerned with death throughout his life, including these early years as a poet.

One of Faulkner's Oxford friends in a conversation before Faulkner received the Nobel Prize told me that in the nineteen-twenties Faulkner said he expected to die young. Phil Stone more than once pointed out that it was odd for Faulkner to ask Stone, some years his senior, to be his executor.

It is possible to be more precise about Faulkner's expectation: In 1924 not long after his twenty-seventh birthday and a little more than a year and a half before he assembled this sonnet cycle for Helen Baird, Faulkner wrote a pertinent letter from Oxford to a friend. Though he has lost the postmaster job he is, he says, not very concerned about how to make a living, and he gives the reason: For nearly a year he has felt a powerful presentiment that he soon will die, not right away but before he is thirty.

Many of Faulkner's poems concern death, the first ten sonnets in this cycle of *Helen: A Courtship* being remarkable exceptions presumably because of their concentration on his love for Helen. And his prose astonishingly often has death as a subject too: early, in "Nympholepsy"; some of the sketches for the New Orleans *Times-Picayune*; *Soldiers' Pay*, from Donald Mahon's death-in-life through to the dust in the shoes of the Rector and Gilligan; *Sartoris*; and *The Sound and the Fury*, featuring the death of Quentin with whom Faulkner so identified himself that as late as July 13, 1950, he could write Joan Williams that she might help him avoid domestic strife by

75

addressing her letters to Quentin Compson, General Delivery, Oxford (though he immediately substituted for Quentin's name that of a character he said would be more certainly unknown to fellow citizens). In the rest of his entire body of fiction death remained an inordinately large element. Rather early an intelligent reviewer of *Doctor Martino and Other Stories* (1934) pointed out: "The title story sounds the pitch of many of these tales and much of Faulkner's work. The theme is that in life we are in the midst of death . . ."[66]

A look at some statistics about Housman's *A Shropshire Lad* helps demonstrate Faulkner's preoccupation. He wrote in "Verse Old and Nascent" that after he had discovered Swinburne at sixteen he had been attracted also to Robinson, Frost, Aldington, and Aiken, but it was in *A Shropshire Lad* he found "the secret after which the moderns course howling like curs on a cold trail in a dark wood . . . Here was reason for being born into a fantastic world: discovering the splendor of fortitude, the beauty of being of the soil like a tree about which fools might howl and which winds of disillusion and death and despair might strip, leaving it bleak, without bitterness; beautiful in sadness."[67] There are sixty-three poems in *A Shropshire Lad*. A quick count shows that forty-seven of them are about death or anticipation of death from one cause or another, including war, execution, suicide. Of the remaining sixteen poems one wishes a soldier well (presumably that he will survive death in battle), eight are about love (unrequited in all but one), six long for home, and one—poem LI—teaches stoicism: A marble statue recommends, "'Courage, lad, 'tis not for long: / Stand, quit you like stone, be strong.'[68] / . . . And I stept out in flesh and bone / Manful like the man of stone." The attraction of Housman's poems, which all his life Faulkner was to quote and recommend to his intimates and buy for them, must have been related to the excessive concern for death he demonstrated in his works, from his poetry through to the end.

He was aware that for him writing those works was a way to deal with death: He made in 1953 an important and explicit statement on the subject, in a July 8 letter to Joan Williams about writing. He said there was an answer, a reason for everything, the single, the most powerful, the most durable way one can tell death "No": "to make something." That opinion is shared by what a later book review said "may be one of the most challenging books of the decade," Ernest Becker, *The Denial of Death* (1974). The reviewer, Anatole Broyard, wrote that to deal with death Becker "has his own suggestion, not as happy as we might irrationally have hoped nor as pessimistic as we might have feared: 'The most that any one of us can seem to do is to fashion something—an object, or ourselves—and drop it into the confusion, make an offering of it, so to speak, to the life force.'" [69]

Faulkner's concern with death is related closely to a theme which became one of his major concepts and received an early statement in lines 11 and 12 of this sonnet, *Helen* IV: "Somewhere a lost green hurt (but better this / Than in rich desolation long forgot)." Faulkner made Harry Wilbourne in *The Wild Palms* put it into the form Faulkner was to use repeatedly in letters, interviews, and speeches, and would say was the central point of *The Wild Palms*: "*between grief and nothing I will take grief.*" That is a matter to take up later.

Most of the time Faulkner displayed notable and admirable stoicism, of the sort recommended by the statue in *A Shropshire Lad*. But it was accompanied by a remarkable amount of melancholy. It is true that often he was entertaining, amused, and amusing. For example, John Crown, talking about the considerable amount of time they had spent together in California, said that Faulkner with him was never gloomy. Joel Sayre told me Faulkner was "one of the pleasantest men to spend time with" that he ever knew. And, as reported above, a letter from Helen Baird Lyman called Faulkner "a truly great companion like the ones you read about but never meet."

Others who knew him well have made much the same report. In the limited number of meetings I had with him, starting in 1948, he was always outgoing and amiable, except for one occasion only.[70] But his letters, such as—just for examples—the many he wrote to Saxe Commins (January 4, 1954: am well but not happy) leave no doubt there was in him a basic layer of melancholy. That it was not confined to his later years is clear from one of her notes of recollections which Judge Lucy Howorth showed me. It records that her husband, Joseph, like herself a fellow student with Faulkner, felt that at the University of Mississippi around the start of the nineteen-twenties Faulkner had "seemed wrapped in despair . . . Joe had never met anyone with such a dark, depressed outlook." Whatever its causes, Faulkner's melancholy probably was in part related to his extreme concern with death.

XV

Though in *Helen* Faulkner dated this sonnet from Paris, September, 1925, he dated a typescript version now at the Berg Collection in March of that year, when he was still at New Orleans. Later the poem appeared in *Contempo* and in a 1932 anthology. Shortened and with the first sentence slightly reworded it became *A Green Bough* XXXIII.

Faulkner's concern over annihilation by death and his attempts to find a way of dealing with it had led him to one possible solution, the stoicism which he says in "Verse Old and Nascent" he had learned from *A Shropshire Lad* (already quoted above): "the splendor of fortitude, the beauty of being of the soil like a tree . . . which winds of disillusion and death and despair might strip, leaving it bleak, without bitterness; beautiful in sadness." Repeating and adapting that image in this sonnet, Faulkner even more somberly presents himself as a tree, one "slain" in "root and branch" and from whose "stalk are stripped the leaves of breath." But even in that extremity of the plight which he inordinately feared, there is one leaf, his heart, which will not die—because of his love. For Faulkner, so concerned by death, to put this sonnet into *Helen: A Courtship* and feature it as the conclusion of the cycle was to give his highest praise to Helen—for inspiring in him a love so strong as to make him immortal.

However much that is a cliché of love poetry, in his other early works connected with Helen Baird, Faulkner had not made the characters which he based on her, however slightly, quite such supporters of life. They were, in fact, sometimes the opposite. Myrtle Monson, according to Faulkner's plans for the novel *Elmer*, would prevent Elmer Hodge from becoming a painter. In light of Faulkner's opinion that creating something was a way to say No to death, Myrtle is for Elmer, with whom Faulkner somewhat identified himself, partly death's handmaiden. Patricia Robyn in *Mosquitoes* is at least lively and she does lead the sculptor to think not only of a golden bell in his heart but of a story related to the theme of this sonnet in *Helen*: A king says he desires "*a thing*"—we later hear, as he does, it is a girl—"*that, dead, remembering it I would cling to this world though it be as a beggar.*" Patricia, however, is also linked to sterility and death. For example, ashore among the mosquitoes the steward, with whom Faulkner partly identifies, knows that Mandeville and safety are to the east, but Patricia insists on going to the west, traditional direction of death, an action which, apart from any symbolism, could have got them killed. But in this sonnet as placed in the cycle, Faulkner concluded *Helen: A Courtship* by giving to Helen Baird without equivocation his fullest literary praise—until he wrote *The Wild Palms*.

The Wild Palms (1939) and the ten novels which preceded it and those which followed are products of Faulkner's momentous change from concentrating his energy on poetry to concentrating it on fiction, a change which happened to coincide with the start of his love for Helen Baird. In the years before he lived at New Orleans he had written short stories but only one had been published and that in a student newspaper. When he reached New Orleans at the beginning of January, 1925, he expected to be there only a few days, until he could arrange freighter passage to Europe. To Phil Stone and to less-close friends he said that his intention was to write poetry primarily, with perhaps a series of prose travel sketches to help pay his way. But he found New Orleans pleasant—for many reasons, including seeing Helen Baird—so he stayed on and soon began to write localized prose sketches which he sold for small but welcome sums to a New Orleans newspaper, the *Times-Picayune*.[71] Those short pieces of fiction vary greatly in quality and interest, but Faulkner found that he enjoyed writing them. Still planning to leave for Europe he began negotiations with the *Times-Picayune* staff for a series of similar sketches he hoped to mail back from his travels. Then he began planning a first novel and soon was writing it with energy and reported joy. In letters to his correspondents in Tennessee and Oklahoma he reported on his progress with the novel and his hopes for it.

Early biographical essays followed the lead of a newspaper article about Faulkner by Louis Cochran, who wrote that Faulkner had half of the manuscript of his first novel, *Soldiers' Pay*, in hand when he went to New Orleans, January, 1925. Cochran had persuaded Phil Stone to check his manuscript for accuracy; so he was believed when he wrote that Faulkner took his novel manuscript with him when he left Oxford for "New Orleans to acquaint himself with the southern literati."[72] The problem with Cochran's statement is that its second half is documentably wrong and Phil Stone knew very well and said more than once that Faulkner had gone to New Orleans only to get passage for Europe and not to visit there among the literati. Stone's not correcting that inaccurate half of Cochran's statement opens the possibility that his letting the other half stand unchallenged does not prove its accuracy.

The only interesting evidence I ever heard that Faulkner had written *Soldiers' Pay* before 1925 was a statement by a woman who told me she remembered that when she visited Oxford shortly before her wedding in 1924 Phil Stone allowed her to read some of Faulkner's typescripts of poetry and prose. Later, when she read the published *Soldiers' Pay*, she realized it was familiar to her. Her testimony deserves serious attention, and her recollection of exactly when it was that Stone let her read among Faulkner's unpublished writings is probably accurate because of her special memory-reinforcing circumstances at the time.

The conflict between her evidence and the contrary reports by Stone and Faulkner himself seemed unresolvable until the Berg Collection acquired the papers Faulkner had got rid of in 1925 at New Orleans, among them a typescript of *Soldiers' Pay*. Embedded in that typescript is a section of several pages bearing independent, presumably earlier, page numbering, which was immediately notable on first going through the typescript. Since then Margaret Yonce has pointed out that the typescript contains not only that apparently once-independent piece but another. One of them is concerned with Januarius Jones, the rector, the rector's son, and Emmy; the other with the drunken soldiers on the train.[73] Professor Yonce's interesting discovery opens the possibility that the bride-to-be, while reading in 1924 among the unpublished Faulkner documents loaned by Stone, could have found the two short stories together sufficient to cause her to tell me that *Soldiers' Pay* seemed familiar to her when it was published. That possibility is congruous with the following: Faulkner said at New Orleans in the third week of February, 1925, that he was thinking out a novel. The next week he went from New Orleans to Oxford for a visit. Two weeks after he returned to New Orleans, he said he was at work on the novel.

The possibility exists therefore that earlier than 1925 he had written the two stories Professor Yonce has identified in the novel's typescript and when he started on his travels had left them in Oxford—for the same load-lightening reason that when he finally did sail for Europe in July of 1925 he left at New Orleans the manuscripts now owned by the Berg Collection.[74] Thinking out a novel after he decided to stay for a time in New Orleans, he perhaps saw the possibilities of building it by joining together the characters in the two short pieces he already had written. From his visit home he perhaps brought them back to New Orleans and began the novel.

In the second week after he had reached New Orleans at the start of 1925, Faulkner had fallen almost by chance into writing his short fictional sketches for the Sunday feature section of the *Times-Picayune*. They had shown him he could write prose of that sort rapidly and with pleasure. He told his Tennessee correspondent he had decided he could no longer write poetry, having passed the emotionally youthful stage necessary for it. He told her that, anyway, he preferred talking to people of various kinds. He had said earlier that the New Orleans streets were filled with stories so that he walked about in the afternoons talking to beggars and policemen and odd types, and in the mornings wrote his newspaper sketches from what he learned on his walks. His pleasure in making the sketches seems to have been important in his deciding to think out and then very energetically write his first novel.

Recent years have seen only one attempt, in a 1977 doctoral dissertation, to revive the idea that before Faulkner reached New Orleans he had written a significant portion of his first novel.[75] A year or so before that dissertation was completed, a conversation after a program on *Soldiers' Pay* arranged by Georgia Institute of Technology had led to hope the dissertation would present significant new evidence. It does not, and additionally argues that Faulkner had written some of his New Orleans sketches before he reached the city in 1925. The two main supports offered for those opinions are that Faulkner could not have written so much as he is thought to have done at New Orleans in 1925 and that some typescripts of the sketches have an unused series title: "SINBAD IN NEW ORLEANS."

Faulkner was capable of writing the short sketches and the novel in his New Orleans months, and his letters to various correspondents make clear that he did so. In his second week at New Orleans he reported he was writing sketches for the *Times-Picayune*, had taken the first to Col. Edmonds, the editor, on the previous day, and had finished a second to submit the next day. After two weeks he had turned in five.

Survival of Sinbad titles does not mean the sketches were written before New Orleans. Faulkner had told Stone and Halle he expected to earn money by writing a series of travel sketches to send back to the United States for newspaper publication. When he found at New Orleans that getting passage on a freighter would take longer than expected, he must have considered it logical to start his travel series there: Sinbad in New Orleans, subsequently, say, Sinbad in Italy, in France. The Sinbad title for the series may have suited his purposes at New Orleans but it obviously did not seem to the *Times-Picayune* staff to suit theirs: A local reference—to Chartres Street—became the newspaper's series title. Faulkner's family owned *The Arabian Nights* and presumably read the voyages of the supreme traveler. In *Mosquitoes* possibly and in *The Wild Palms* specifically Faulkner brought up one of Sinbad's most famous adventures, with the Old Man of the Sea. Faulkner at New Orleans could have put his Sinbad title on the first sketches he wrote and submitted to the *Times-Picayune*; there was plenty of time for the newspaper to have Faulkner replace the titles and make revisions: Almost two weeks passed between Faulkner's writing and submitting the last of his first five sketches and the newspaper's publication of the first of them, which was followed on successive Sundays by other sketches for which

Sinbad-titled typescripts survive.[76] The year 1925, in New Orleans, does seem to have been the time when Faulkner really began his change from what he called "failed poet" to successful novelist.

Of the first three novels which Faulkner worked on, two drew from his relationship with Helen Baird before her marriage to Guy Lyman. In the years between 1927, when he published *Mosquitoes* four days before the Lymans' wedding, and 1939, when he published *The Wild Palms* in which he drew partially on Helen for the main character, Faulkner wrote most of his best novels. During that dozen years he saw Helen and Guy Lyman occasionally and maintained his friendship with Helen through an exchange of infrequent phone calls and letters, some of which are in the Wisdom Collection of Faulkner at Tulane. He often visited with the Lymans, Helen told me, and he was with them now and then among the dinner guests of mutual friends in New Orleans. He sometimes went hunting with Guy Lyman. Faulkner was a guest of the Lymans near Picayune, Mississippi, at a vacation and hunting place where they kept a notably large number of hunting dogs.

Once when the Lymans invited him to Picayune Faulkner brought with him the manuscript of *Absalom, Absalom!* (1936). During much of the writing of that novel Faulkner was seriously upset by the death of his brother Dean in the crash of the plane Faulkner had supplied. In an earlier, also especially troubled time for him—1931—Faulkner had traveled restlessly and had carried along the manuscript-in-progress of *Light in August*, one part of which he mislaid and one part he lost, according to what Anthony Buttitta and a New York editor told me in interviews.[77] At the Lymans' place near Picayune Faulkner had a similar experience with *Absalom, Absalom!*. During that visit he began drinking heavily enough to become quite ill. Guy Lyman arranged for an ambulance, and after it had taken Faulkner away, Helen said, she learned the manuscript for *Absalom, Absalom!* had been left behind; so she went back to get it, and mailed it off wrapped in an old cover of one of the Lyman children's Mother Goose books. A

Helen Baird, self portrait

friend of the Lymans told me that Faulkner, grateful and apologetic, soon presented Guy Lyman with a horse.

In *The Wild Palms* Faulkner drew on Helen for several of the characteristics of his fictional Charlotte Rittenmeyer, whom he seems to me to present as admirable, which is contrary to the judgment in most published criticism of the novel. He also drew in detail on his recollections of his emotions, which presumably intensified his fictional presentation of Harry Wilbourne, who meets and falls in love with the fictional Charlotte in New Orleans at the age of Faulkner when he had met Helen Baird there and had fallen in love. Harry loses Charlotte, and Faulkner had lost Helen, though not by death. Faulkner admiringly modeled Charlotte on Helen's person and personality—color of eyes, complexion, figure, childhood burn injury, directness, vivacity, compelling attractiveness—and on some of her manner and mannerisms as well as activities and interests, such as her making small salable figures. In partially using recollections of Helen while creating Charlotte, aged about twenty-five in the novel, Faulkner did not draw just on the young woman he had asked to marry him in 1925 but also on the somewhat older Helen whom he knew in the years after her marriage. Her aunt, Mrs. Martin, pointed out to me some of the ways the fictional Charlotte was similar to her niece, but Helen and Faulkner never had any such relationship as that of Charlotte and Harry Wilbourne nor did Helen leave her husband and children; Faulkner with Charlotte in *The Wild Palms* did once again in a single respect what he had done with Myrtle Monson in *Elmer* and Patricia Robyn in *Mosquitoes*: He made a fictional figure partly formed by drafts on other literary works and set her in an imagined plot to serve his purposes and not to record the real Helen.

In the opinion of Helen's close friend, Ann Farnsworth, though Faulkner certainly did not base the plot of *The Wild*

Palms on Helen's life he put enough of her physical and personal characteristics and her expressions into the fictional Charlotte to explain completely a statement which Helen made to her in 1939: When Ann Farnsworth read that *The Wild Palms* had been published, she told Helen she saw that Faulkner had brought out a new book. "Don't read it," Helen replied. "It's no good." As soon as Ann Farnsworth did read *The Wild Palms*, she says, she fully understood the reason for that response: Helen obviously realized Faulkner had given Charlotte several of her own characteristics.

Faulkner seems to have written *The Wild Palms* to deal with three significant emotional losses and simultaneously to examine a major maneuver in his life-long effort to cope with his concern for death.

Meta Wilde remembers that Faulkner wrote some of the material of *The Wild Palms* while she was living in one of the cottages at Normandie Village in Hollywood near the beginning of the Sunset Strip. She lived there for the ten months before her marriage to Wolfgang Rebner on April 5, 1937. What Faulkner wrote then possibly was the unpublished short story which survives in holograph and typescript at the University of Virginia and some preliminary work on the novel. The story is similar to part of the novel's opening section, concentrating on the dead-in-life doctor, neighbor of the younger man and woman who rent his cottage. One critic has written that *The Wild Palms* is set in the Pascagoula of Helen Baird. Actually its Mississippi Gulf Coast sections are set in the Pascagoula of Estelle—and William Faulkner, during the first summer of their marriage, 1929, when they lived there in a vacation cottage on the beach. Their real next door neighbors at that cottage and their relationship with them supplied a few elements of the situation of the fictional Harry and Charlotte with the doctor and his wife in the novel, judging by what the survivor of the neighboring real couple told me.

And probably when Faulkner wrote the short story which contains material he worked into part of the opening of the novel, his thoughts were much on his wife: He was in love with Meta but felt bound by his marriage.

When Meta, realizing she and Faulkner were not going to marry, went ahead with her own life and married Wolfgang Rebner, Faulkner entered a condition about which in later letters to Meta and to Joan Williams he used the word "heartbreak." He also later explicitly stated that he wrote *The Wild Palms* to deal with that heartbreak: After what he had to assume was the final loss of Meta, he used the short story in writing the novel, but went, of course, far beyond it, and in new directions.

This was not the first time Faulkner produced a literary work in such a period of loss. A decade before, on March 14, 1927—ten days after Helen married Guy Lyman—Faulkner dated an unpublished sonnet typescript, now in the Rowan Oak Papers at the University of Virginia. Titled "Admonishes His Heart," it begins, "Be still, my heart, be still, since you must grieve . . ." Faulkner drew much of the poem from *The Shropshire Lad*, XLVIII, at times almost directly quoting, but for Housman's sorrow about the entire universe Faulkner substituted his personal loss of the woman he loved: "Think on the long cold years ere beauty's wings / Made light within my air . . ." The sestet begins, "Once there was lightless time: I had not birth / ---Be still, my heart, be still: you break in vain . . ." It ends:

> There was beauty then, and grief and pain
> But I lay close and dark and richly dearth.
> Why did I wake? When shall I sleep again?

After a period of hospitalization, work on films, and finishing *The Unvanquished*, Faulkner dated the first page of the surviving holograph manuscript of *The Wild Palms* September 15, 1937.[78] Shortly after that, when Meta and Wolfgang Rebner returned to New York from their honeymoon in Europe, Faulkner met them at the dock.

Work on the novel went slowly, one deterrent to progress being the severe burning of his back at a New York hotel in November, 1937. Meta remembers that when he invited her and her husband to have dinner at the Algonquin, they arrived to find him bedridden because of that burn, and in such pain that they left quickly to give him rest. The pain persisted, and it was February 13, 1938, before Faulkner dated the beginning of his holograph of the fourth chapter. By the middle of June he had finished the holograph version.

In the novel as it grew Charlotte became a figure which, as noted above, too much published criticism has considered reprehensible: She abandons her husband and two children, she takes Harry away from his proposed profession, and she seems to many critics to consider sex not just central to life but the only significant thing in it. In addition she wants an abortion at a time when it was not only severely opposed but illegal in the United States; a situation difficult for readers to understand today when the newspapers are full of a serious question about abortions: Should the federal government continue to provide them at no cost.

Surely a major reason so many critics still consider Charlotte totally defective is that, trapped by conventionality, they cannot believe Faulkner would do anything in writing his outstanding fiction which they would not do if they wrote fiction. They assume Faulkner wanted us to dislike Charlotte and they often assume we are to admire the convict in the contrapuntal sections, "Old Man"—and surely are wrong on both counts.

The convict in *The Wild Palms* is not the first of Faulkner's characters whom the majority of critics erroneously, it would seem, have decided Faulkner expected them to admire. Many admire Benjy Compson in *The Sound and the Fury* because they feel he is innocent—and besides, he is handicapped. Many admire Addie in *As I Lay Dying* because she is a mother and is more driving than most of her family. Many admire the convict in *The Wild Palms* because to them he seems a healthy, silent nature boy in admirable contrast to those decadent city types, Charlotte and Harry. But Faulkner, unlike many who write about his works, was not conventional and as a genius it would have been unbearably painful for him to have tried to be. He took chances with his innovative forms and with his style—and with his concepts of character: Benjy is not different from the rest of his unlucky family, we just are not angry at him because it is even more obvious with him, an idiot, than with his parents and brothers that he cannot help being totally selfish. Addie Bundren is actually unattractive in spite of her usually misunderstood and repeatedly quoted remark about the ineffectiveness of words (in an effective novel which is nothing but words—except for one small drawing of a coffin); her major act of motherhood is to drive the central character, her son, into the state insane asylum.[79] The convict in *The Wild Palms*, as excellent studies have pointed out—unfortunately without much effect on some of Faulkner's critics—is by no means admirable or meant to be, for he is an emotional cripple and represents a repudiation of life which Faulkner found appalling. With Charlotte, Faulkner seems to have done what he did with Benjy, Addie, and the convict—but in reverse.

Though in very recent years some criticism is much more favorable to Charlotte, many of the established and popularly influential critics still consider her reprehensible for the reasons mentioned above. But I believe Faulkner in his complex treatment of her, though not conventional and not making things easy for her as a fictional character or for himself as a creator of fiction, presented her as admirable in a way requiring some discussion.

The Wild Palms is a rich and complex work which in spite of its rejection by so many has been greatly admired by some.[80] A few excellent studies of it are available, important among them, because of its scope and quality, is Thomas L. McHaney's book-length examination, *William Faulkner's The Wild Palms*.[81] Forgoing that rich complexity of the novel, this biographical essay on Faulkner's relationship with Helen Baird should make only one point, which is in disagreement with views expressed by some of those excellent examinations as well as by the greater number of popularly influential studies.

McHaney effectively points out Faulkner's detailed connections between his characters, Charlotte Rittenmeyer and Harry Wilbourne, and the sinners suffering at the seventh circle and elsewhere in Dante's *Inferno*. But I believe Faulkner put important subtleties into his presentation of Charlotte as what convention would call a sinner. If he had thought she was reprehensible he would have been defeating the purpose which Harry serves at the end of the novel by rejecting suicide in order to keep alive the memory of Charlotte, deciding to live on in grief rather than accepting obliteration of his grief, himself, and his memory of her. Faulkner not only told his publisher that Harry's decision—between grief and nothing to take grief—was "the theme of the whole book"[82] but obviously respected Harry's making it. For Faulkner simultaneously to admire Harry for keeping Charlotte's memory alive at great cost and to consider Charlotte a defective person not worth remembering would make no sense. In spite of her unconventional behavior, Charlotte is estimably striving to be intensely alive. She also demonstrates what Faulkner, in the letter to Joan Williams mentioned above, said was the best and most enduring way to say No to death: Charlotte understands that the way to do it is "to make something."

Very near death, in great pain, Charlotte says to Harry, "'Jesus, we had fun, didn't we, bitching, and making things?'"[83]

On the last page of Harry's appearance in the novel, when he is about to say his crucially significant final words about grief and nothing, he says that what he wants to keep alive is "remembering, the body, the broad thighs[84] and the hands that liked bitching and making things." (p. 324) The "bitching" is saying Yes to being alive, the making things is saying No to death.

Charlotte's concern with love-making is probably so great because people while involved in it can most easily be fully alive just for the moment, without thought of past or future. Charlotte is not nymphomaniacally uncontrolled; unlike the Buckners she refuses to make love during the six weeks she and Harry have no privacy at the Utah mine. (p. 192–93, 197) Popularly believed critics have said that Charlotte is acting in a literary tradition of being overly "romantic," and is eager to escape from "domesticity," the "bourgeois world." Faulkner presents her as motivated by more than such common conditions. The novel specifically shows Harry realizing that there is "a part of her . . . which did not even love love." (p. 90)

Walter Pater—one in a group of writers, including Anatole France and Henri Bergson, whom Faulkner liked and who had related thoughts—wrote the most quoted epigrammatic remark about the desirability of living intensely, as though burning with a hard, gem-like flame. Faulkner sometimes mentioned "flame," one time speaking the word directly in connection with Helen Baird not just using it in print as he did, for example, in *Mosquitoes*, which he dedicated to her.[85] Mrs. Martin, Helen's aunt, told me that in the summer of 1926, when Helen was not at Pascagoula, Faulkner came to call for the first time. He said he was in love with her niece. He then, with intensity, asked Mrs. Martin how she thought of Helen. Mrs. Martin intelligently responded by asking how Faulkner himself thought of her. He replied, "As an amber flame."

Though he used that concept in *Mosquitoes*, which he was writing that summer, he used it much more, and more significantly, in *The Wild Palms*. He repeatedly emphasized Charlotte's "yellow" eyes and their effect on Harry. (Though one biography has said that Helen Baird Lyman had "light blue eyes,"[86] her eyes were brownish and, as her friends have put it, had "a decidedly yellow cast"—adding another link between Helen and Charlotte.) By more than just the proximity of colors Charlotte's eyes are related to the "amber flame" of Faulkner's talk with Helen's aunt—by "flame" as well: Charlotte's "yellow eyes" at one point showed a "fierce affirmation . . . in which [Harry] seemed to blunder and fumble like a moth." (p. 87)

Pater said to live like a flame. "Promethean fire" is, according to an encyclopedia, "The vital principle; the fire with which Prometheus quickened into life his clay images."[87] Zeus had employed Prometheus to make men and women of earth and water. Concerned for their well-being, Prometheus stole fire for them from the Gods. By giving human beings the flame of life he was their benefactor, and the people of Greece honored him at annual festivals by a race with torches. Charlotte Rittenmeyer gave the flame of life to Harry Wilbourne in this novel about life and death. Having been in a dead existence until they met, by her strength Harry came to live, at the jail, with fierce joy. He simultaneously demonstrated what Charlotte had taught him and honored her by refusing Rat's cyanide pill, to live and to keep her memory alive.

The judgment and punishment systems of both Olympus and Dante's Inferno were operated by similar Higher Powers. By them Prometheus was judged a sinner and punished by great pain, and so was Charlotte.

Charlotte goes against whatever Powers have made too many human beings dead though still alive. Faulkner shows us samples in this novel, beginning with the first character we see, the beach-side doctor whose remembering to take home his flashlight prompts Harry, by then a connoisseur, to observe that *"he probably never forgot anything in his life except that he was alive once, must have been born alive at least."* (p. 281) Others in the novel are dead-in-life or—the convict in the contrapuntal story—essentially unborn.

Charlotte took unpleasant actions (leaving Rat and their children) in her attempt to defeat whatever Powers have made it impossible for us to live intensely every moment "'not just to eat and evacuate and sleep warm so we can get up and eat and evacuate in order to sleep warm again!'" (p. 118–19) Charlotte, like the protagonist of Shelley's *Prometheus Unbound*, acts in opposition to omnipotent force and in the interest of what Shelley calls "heaven-oppressed mortality."

Though she succeeded as a teacher of Harry, many readers obviously see her as failing to achieve her goal. But Faulkner fully established himself by repeated public statements to be one who knew that everyone fails and that the only judgment we should make concerns the quality of the goal at which the failure aimed. If, as Faulkner said, Thomas Wolfe was the most successful novelist among his contemporaries because, failing like the rest, he had tried for more, certainly Charlotte would in Faulkner's opinion be a remarkable success—as he obviously demonstrated she was by Harry's admiration for her and his own admiration for the Harry she created. Faulkner repeatedly said that life is motion, and some writers on *The Wild Palms* have felt that Faulkner must have disliked Charlotte because they think he created her as one who believes in stasis, opposes motion. It seems possible to argue that he did not, witness her pleasure and excitement when the Wisconsin buck springs away, "'That's what I was trying to make!' she cried. 'Not the animals, the dogs and deer and horses: the motion, the speed.'" (p. 99–100)

Charlotte—whose name as the feminine form of Charles

includes among its meanings "noble-spirited," who admirably shows "almost unbearable honesty" (p. 109) and even in the extremity of pain urges Harry to leave her and escape arrest—has not only, when "making something," been making figures of modest artistic value; she has been making herself (and Harry). Becker, expanding in *Denial of Death* the same idea which Faulkner had expressed in a letter, specifies that in saying No to death by making something the something need not be an object but can be oneself. It is possible that Faulkner's thought included that option and so offset the frequent objections that Charlotte does not make great art. Besides, if Faulkner and Becker meant that what we have to make is good art, the opportunity to use their method of saying No to death would be too restricted to be of interest.

The goal Charlotte set herself as "an apostate from convention" (p. 85) contributes to the condition which Harry suddenly recognizes as he says, "*Why, she's alone.*" (p. 82) Charlotte is completely unconventional, and this is not a novel to use to support the belief that "community" is Faulkner's favorite subject—though here as in a number of Faulkner's works the community does play a part, wanting to lynch Rat because he tries to make a plea for Harry. The bailiff tells the judge that the community is only at the tar-and-feather stage (as it was with Hightower in *Light in August*) and not at the killing stage (as it was in that novel with Joe Christmas, or in *Sanctuary* when it destroyed Lee Goodwin, or *Intruder in the Dust* where the community would have killed the innocent Lucas Beauchamp except for the efforts of two young boys and an elderly woman almost as unconventional as Charlotte Rittenmeyer).

Charlotte's unconventionality and all its accompaniments are why Harry admired her and loved her so much he wanted to preserve her memory. Faulkner had something to say about love which relates to that. Pointing out, in a letter to Marjorie

Lyons about the reporter in *Pylon*, that we sometimes choose a love too large for us, he said of the reporter, "That's what he did. Tragic, sad love; but better than nothing."[88] After adding that to love is better than to be loved, Faulkner drew Mrs. Lyons' attention to Harry Wilbourne for his decision about grief and nothing. Harry's love is, like the reporter's, tragic, sad love, but that Faulkner created and admired Harry's decision to live because of it represents a remarkable change in Faulkner between the late nineteen-thirties when he wrote *The Wild Palms* and the middle nineteen-twenties when he first knew Helen Baird and wrote *Mayday*, the other hand-lettered and hand-bound booklet which, like *Helen: A Courtship*, he gave to her in token of his love.

In *Mayday* Sir Galwyn comes in the end of the booklet to a stream at which, like Harry Wilbourne of *The Wild Palms*, he can decide whether to accept grief, by crossing the stream and starting again through life, or to accept annihilation—nothing—by joining in the stream the girl whom Saint Francis identifies for him as Sister Death. Sir Galwyn chooses to drown in the stream. Harry, in Wisconsin fairly early in *The Wild Palms*, thinks with some desire about drowning in the lake, but as his time with Charlotte and his tutelage by her example continue he achieves, at the end of his part in the book, the decision which Faulkner liked so much he cited it often during the remaining nearly quarter-century of his life.

What Faulkner presented about life and death in *The Wild Palms* will not satisfy the religious, who already have much more optimistic conceptions of mortality than Faulkner apparently ever was able to achieve. His best way to try to ease his concern with death remained sufficiently unoptimistic to make him all his life poignantly aware of time's passage. Sonnet 116, Meta Wilde has told me, was the poem by Shakespeare which Faulkner most often quoted to her. It says that "Love is not love / Which alters when it alteration finds." "O no! it is an ever fixed mark . . ." For "Love's not Time's fool." G. Wilson Knight has written in a study of Shakespeare: "The poet must say, and we applaud him for saying it, 'Love's not Time's fool' (116), but he fears, and so do we, that it may be."[89] And there is a sorrowful view of time in a poem Faulkner quoted much of his life, orally and in letters, and which Meta Wilde said was the poem of all Faulkner quoted to her which he quoted most frequently: Joyce's "Watching the Needleboats at San Sabba," with its moving evocation of transience, the "young hearts crying" vainly, the "wind that passes" which will return no more.

That concern with the disappearing past and with memory, which enriches much of Faulkner's fiction, obviously was a part of a visit Faulkner made late in his life back to the places where he had written his first published novels, and had fallen in love with Helen Baird. In 1955 when Jean Stein was at the Mississippi location for the film *Baby Doll*, Faulkner and she went to New Orleans and Pascagoula, near the end of the year. Walking on the almost deserted Pascagoula beach, they met Helen Baird Lyman, also out for a walk, and talked briefly. Later when I told Jean Stein that Faulkner had once proposed marriage to Helen Baird, she said that she had felt in the air something out of the ordinary during the brief conversation that day at Pascagoula but had never known what it was.

Two years earlier, in a letter to Meta Wilde, on May 15, 1953, Faulkner had expressed what surely was a part of his private thought during that meeting, thirty years after he first saw Helen and proposed marriage and began gathering his sonnet cycle for her: "Change in people: the saddest thing of all, division, separation, all left is the remembering, the dream, until you almost believe that anything beautiful is nothing else but dream." Helen's own, apparently similar, feeling about that chance meeting she expressed almost immediately by starting to paint this portrait, which she never finished, and in which Faulkner appears much older than he actually looked when he and she met on the empty winter beach, the last time they would ever see each other.

Unfinished portrait of Faulkner by Helen Baird Lyman, 1955

NOTES

[1] (New York: Random House, 1974.)

[2] Joseph Blotner, ed., *Selected Letters of William Faulkner* (New York, Random House, 1977).

[3] *Sewanee Review*, Spring, 1977, pp. [218]–234.

[4] (New Haven and London: Yale University Press, 1978.)

[5] (Lincoln and London: University of Nebraska Press, 1979.)

[6] (Baltimore and London: The Johns Hopkins University Press, 1980.)

[7] Holograph, on verso of p. 269 of the typescript. See illustration here, courtesy of the Alderman Library, University of Virginia. Joan St. C. Crane and Carl Petersen gave invaluable help with Faulkner's holograph, always difficult enough without the added barrier of cancellation of all the lines.

[8] Joseph Blotner, *Faulkner: A Biography*, p. 439.

[9] *Ibid.*, p. 543. Discussed in William Boozer, *William Faulkner's First Book: The Marble Faun Fifty Years Later* (Memphis: Pigeon Roost Press, 1974), pp. 30–32.

[10] At Alderman Library, University of Virginia.

[11] Malcolm Cowley, "Faulkner Was Wrong About 'Sanctuary,'" review of William Faulkner, *Sanctuary: The Original Text*, ed. Noel Polk (New York: Random House, 1981), New York *Times Book Review*, Feb. 22, 1981, pp. 9, 25.

[12] "A Portrait of Elmer," Joseph Blotner, ed., *Uncollected Stories of William Faulkner* (New York: Random House, 1979), pp. 610–641.

[13] At Alderman Library, University of Virginia.

[14] William Faulkner, *Mayday* (Notre Dame, Indiana: University of Notre Dame Press, 1978), ed. Carvel Collins, p. 17–18.

[15] Faulkner's use of *Jurgen* in *Mayday* is discussed, *ibid.*, pp. 21–23.

[16] Though it is said Faulkner started the novel later, a friend in Paris has reported he was at work on it there in 1925.

[17] Cleanth Brooks, *William Faulkner: Toward Yoknapatawpha and Beyond*, p. 60.

[18] *Ibid.*, p. 377.

[19] Carvel Collins, ed., *William Faulkner: Early Prose and Poetry* (Boston: Little, Brown and Co., 1962), pp. 101–103.

[20] Critics have noted that *Mosquitoes* also bears similarities to Huxley's *Chrome Yellow*.

[21] Critics began to notice the debt of Talliaferro in *Mosquitoes* to Prufrock at least as early as Frederick L. Gwynn's "Faulkner's Prufrock—and Other Observations," *Journal of English and Germanic Philology*, January, 1953, pp. 63–70.

[22] Critics have linked the drunken scene near the end of *Mosquitoes* to Joyce's *Ulysses*. Flaubert's *The Temptation of St. Anthony* may have contributed to that scene.

[23] Mary M. Dunlap, "Sex and the Artist in *Mosquitoes*," *Mississippi Quarterly*, Summer, 1969, pp. 190–206.

[24] Joseph Blotner, *Faulkner: A Biography*, pp. 419, 436, 437, 507, 509, 518.

[25] Quoted in Stuart Shoffman, "Life and times from a newsweekly alum," Los Angeles *Times*, December 7, 1980, book section, p. 4.

[26] Eula Varner—in the first volume of the Snopes trilogy—is such a character.

[27] Cleanth Brooks, *William Faulkner: Toward Yoknapatawpha and Beyond*, p. 55.

[28] *William Faulkner: Early Prose and Poetry*, pp. 13–16.

[29] Carvel Collins, ed., *William Faulkner: New Orleans Sketches* (New York: Random House, 1968), pp. 46, 53.

[30] Lewis P. Simpson, "Sex & History: Origins of Faulkner's Apocrypha," in Evans Harrington and Ann Abadie, eds., *The Maker and the Myth: Faulkner and Yoknapatawpha 1977* (Jackson: University Press of Mississippi, 1977), pp. 45–46.

[31] George A. Buttrick, ed., *The Interpreter's Dictionary of the Bible* (New York: Abingdon Press, 1962), Vol. I, 4, p. 290.

[32] George A. Buttrick, ed., *The Interpreter's Bible* (New York: Abingdon-Cokesbury Press, 1952), p. 494.

[33] At Alderman Library, University of Virginia.

[34] Noel Polk, "Introduction," William Faulkner, *The Marionettes*, (Charlottesville: University Press of Virginia, 1977), p. xxv.

[35] *Ibid.*, pp. xxviii–xxx.

[36] George Moore, *Memoirs of My Dead Life* (London: William Heinemann, 1921), p. 317.

[37] "The Hill," *William Faulkner: Early Prose and Poetry*, pp. 90–92, 132.

[38] In Faulkner Special Issue, ed. James B. Meriwether, *Mississippi Quarterly*, Summer, 1973. Reprinted in James B. Meriwether, ed., *A Faulkner Miscellany* (Jackson: University Press of Mississippi, 1974), pp. 149–155.

[39] George Moore, *Memoirs of My Dead Life*, p. 140. A view opposing the romanticism of Moore's account of nympholepsy appears in *A High Place* by James Branch Cabell, whose works Faulkner read and drew on—and sometimes discussed with his New Orleans friend, John McClure. There a chief character says: "It is droll that a little color and glitter and a few plump curves, seen once and very briefly, should be able to make all other things not quite worth troubling about. But the farce is old. They used to call us nympholepts;

and they fabled that the beauty which robbed us of all normal human joys was divine . . . It suffices that I loved you in this pre-eminently ridiculous fashion . . ." (New York: Robert M. McBride & Co., 1923), p. 266.

[40] Another small sample from Faulkner's poetry is the line "A caught breath, flash of limbs in the myrtles apart." It first appeared in a poem he wrote at New Haven in 1921, with "An Old Man Says:" as its title. Later in the 'twenties he gave to Katherine Lawless an untitled and somewhat revised version which still retained that nympholeptic line, as did other versions now at the University of Texas from the Stones' house, at the University of Virginia, and in print in *Contempo* and at least two other publications under the title "I Will Not Weep for Youth."

[41] William Faulkner, "Sherwood Anderson," Dallas *Morning News*, April 26, 1925, Part III, p. 7. Reprinted: James B. Meriwether, ed., *Princeton University Library Chronicle*, Spring, 1957, p. 93.

[42] George Moore, *Memoirs of My Dead Life*, p. 81.

[43] *Ibid.*, p. 82. Faulkner was to speak of himself as an artist vagrant long after he had acquired a family, a house with acreage, a farm, and—according to a tally he once worked up for Meta Wilde—a large number of dependents.

[44] *Ibid.*, pp. 119, 142, 145, 189, 205.

[45] Meta Carpenter Wilde and Orin Borsten, (New York: Simon and Schuster, 1976).

[46] Milton Britten, "There's Even Something Distinctive about William Faulkner's Tobacco," Memphis *Press-Scimitar*, April 28, 1955, n.p.

[47] George Moore, *Memoirs of My Dead Life*, pp. 360–61.

[48] John McClure, "Literature and Less," New Orleans *Times-Picayune*, June 20, 1926, Sunday feature section, p. 4, col. 1.

[49] Joseph Blotner, *William Faulkner's Library—A Catalogue* (Charlottesville: University Press of Virginia, 1964).

[50] *Ibid.*, p. 7.

[51] Reprinted in James B. Meriwether and Michael Millgate, eds., *Lion in the Garden: Interviews with William Faulkner, 1926–1962* (New York: Random House, 1968) pp. [215]–231 and [237]–256.

[52] The legible poems in the partially burned sheaf of "1923" appear in *A Green Bough* as VI, VIII, XIV, XVII, XVIII, XXVI, XXVII, XXVIII, XXIX, XXX, XLI, XLIII. Any or all could have been written well before 1923, as, for example, was XVII in a different version dated 1920. See footnote 64, below.

[53] David Minter, *William Faulkner: His Life and Work*, p. 162.

[54] Meta Carpenter Wilde and Orin Borsten, *A Loving Genlteman*, p. 77.

[55] David Minter, *William Faulkner: His Life and Work*, p. 163.

[56] Joan Williams has also effectively made the same point in her "Twenty Will Not Come Again," *Atlantic Monthly*, May, 1980, p. 63.

[57] Harvey Breit, "Talk with Conrad Aiken," New York *Times Book Review*, July 31, 1949, p. 10.

[58] Robert N. Linscott, "Faulkner without Fanfare," *Esquire*, July, 1963, p. 38. A statement about *The Phoenix and the Turtle* by G. Wilson Knight may partially explain Faulkner's lifelong quoting of it, especially in times of trou-

ble: "The main point to remember is that the Phoenix suggests a difficult, tragic and yet victorious experience." *The Mutual Flame* (London: Methuen, 1962), p. 155.

[59] Faulkner's grandaunt, Mrs. Walter B. McLean, said in August, 1951, that once when she was reading Virginia Woolf's *Orlando* and told Faulkner she was finding it difficult, he urged her to put it aside because there was no reason to struggle over difficult reading, that some works are for some people and others for others. He then added, she told me, that people should not try to read books which do not appeal to them almost at once.

[60] Frederick Chapman, ed. (New York: Dodd, Mead & Co., 1922), p. 113.

[61] Now in the Faulkner Collections at the Alderman Library, University of Virginia. It has been published in Joseph Blotner ed., *Selected Letters of William Faulkner* (New York: Random House, 1977), pp. 19–20.

[62] Robert Wilson has reproduced the holograph as an illustration, opposite page 54 of his book, *Modern Book Collecting* (New York: Alfred A. Knopf, 1980).

[63] The happier aspects of this cluster of elements appear in two letters Faulkner wrote a quarter-century later, in 1950, to Joan Williams, January 23 and October 13.

[64] The booklet is now in the excellent Faulkner collection of L. D. Brodsky. It is described, with photographic reproductions of two openings, in Robert W. Hamblin & Louis Daniel Brodsky, *Selections from the William Faulkner Collection of Louis Daniel Brodsky: A Descriptive Catalogue* (Charlottesville: The University Press of Virginia, 1979), pp. 31–34.

[65] Quoted by Richard Locke, review of *Gravity's Rainbow*, New York *Times Book Review*, March 11, 1973, p. [1].

[66] Fred T. Marsh, "A Miscellany of Faulkner Stories," New York *Herald Tribune Books*, April 15, 1934. When it appeared, this review was a revelation to me about Faulkner's obvious compulsive concern with death—obvious, that is, when the reviewer had pointed it out.

[67] *Double Dealer*, April, 1925. Reprinted in "Appendix" of *William Faulkner: Early Prose and Poetry*, p. 117. A facsimile of a typescript of the essay, dated "October, 1924," is in William Faulkner, *Mississippi Poems*, ed. Joseph Blotner, facsimile edition (Oxford, Mississippi: Yoknapatawpha Press, 1979), pp. 39–51.

[68] Presumably Housman here made a pessimistic, ironical variation from I Corinthians 16:13, "Watch ye, stand fast in the faith, quit you like men, be strong."

[69] Anatole Broyard, "The Suction of the Infinite: II," New York *Times*, May 28, 1974, p. 33. A review of Ernest Becker, *The Denial of Death* (New York: Free Press, 1974).

[70] Faulkner seemed to go out of his way to be pleasant whenever I saw him in Oxford, except once, when he was so withdrawn that his stepson, Malcolm Franklin, said the family was worried and that Faulkner seemed to Malcolm to be "in male menopause." While reading a few hundred Faulkner letters after his death I realized that those written around the time of that single

sad visit were his gloomiest. In one of them he even wrote that he never in his life had been so despondent. During later meetings he was again amiable: in Oxford, at the marriage of his daughter, Jill, and during a day or so following the wedding; in Massachusetts, at my house in Lincoln; and in New York, after an award ceremony, during dinner at Jean Stein's, and on a walk in Manhattan. Surprisingly, it was during the days of the visit at his house in Oxford when he was so withdrawn, unsocial, and seemed especially melancholy that he volunteered by far the greatest amount of information about his fiction which he ever gave to me. During several talks in earlier years, starting in 1948, he only occasionally had spoken of his works, most of the conversation being about horses, sailing, and farming. But during the visit when he was so unsocial he, oddly enough, in a long burst of monologue on his front porch told me about real people and places he had used in his fiction. Perhaps not so oddly, though, judging now by his letters and in view of his great concern about annihilation, for he may have been so especially melancholy as to have wanted even such matters somehow not to disappear entirely.

[71] Reprinted in *William Faulkner: New Orleans Sketches.*

[72] "William Faulkner: A Personal Sketch," Memphis *Commercial Appeal,* November 6, 1932, Sunday feature section, p. 4. Reprinted in James B. Meriwether, "Early Notices of Faulkner By Phil Stone And Louis Cochran," *Mississippi Quarterly,* Summer, 1964, p. 145.

[73] "The Composition of *Soldiers' Pay,*" *Mississippi Quarterly,* Summer, 1980, pp. 293–304. Parenthetically, this extremely useful article is trapped in its ninth footnote into an improbable speculation about the timing of some of Faulkner's writing by the misconception in published biography, noted above, that Faulkner finished *Soldiers' Pay* in May, 1925, and at once turned it over for final typing in Oxford.

[74] All published discussions which I have seen of the Faulkner papers acquired by the Berg Collection in 1971 assume that the postmarked date on the box in which they had been preserved is a significant aid in dating the composition of the papers. But some of them were written after that date, and there is every likelihood that the papers had merely been stored in that box at New Orleans rather than mailed there in it. The box probably received its postmark when Phil Stone mailed some of the items which Faulkner's letters from New Orleans occasionally asked him to send.

[75] Leland Holcombe Cox, Jr., *Sinbad in New Orleans: Early Short Fiction by William Faulkner,* doctoral dissertation, University of South Carolina, 1977.

[76] The surfacing at the Berg Collection a decade ago of typescripts for seven (and a few lines from an eighth) among sixteen sketches Faulkner wrote for the New Orleans *Times-Picayune* during his transition in 1925 from poetry to fiction makes possible a better text than could be made when the only available sources were the printed sketches in the newspaper. But a new edition would still suffer from the fact that for more than half of the *Times-Picayune* sketches the only available text is still the newspaper's. And though the Berg Collection's typescripts would be extremely useful, they, along with

the typescript setting copy used by the *Double Dealer* when it published "New Orleans," offer editing problems which this dissertation has not yet solved. A sample: Which should control the text of the sketch titled "New Orleans" if a new edition were prepared, the typescript setting copy now at Tulane in the Wisdom Collection of Faulkner or the version printed in the *Double Dealer*? The printed version contains a section—"The Sailor"— which is not in the typescript setting copy, and it places the subheads at the center of the pages though the typescript begins each subhead at the left margin, which the dissertation believes should be the format for any new edition because it gives the piece greater unity. But Faulkner obviously had something to do with the text between typescript setting copy and printed page—he added "The Sailor." He then also may have proposed to move, or agreed with his friends at the *Double Dealer* to move, the subheads to the center. So would it be proper, as the dissertation proposes, for new editions to include "The Sailor" from the despised "journalistic" printed source but for the sake of purity to use the typescript's left-margin placement of the subheads—especially if one notes that when Faulkner hand-made in 1926 a gift booklet for Mrs. Estelle Franklin from this "New Orleans" piece he himself hand-lettered the subheads at the center of the pages, where the dissertation feels they conflict with the artist's intention? Petty example, and selected because a neater quandry than most; but other textual problems remain here. And would it be proper or just novel to give new editions of the sixteen *Times-Picayune* sketches and the one from the *Double Dealer* the overall title *Sinbad in New Orleans* when that title appeared on only four of the seventeen and was eliminated before any were published? *Sinbad in New Orleans* also seems a questionable title for a volume in which one of the stories takes place up-country, in a setting like that of north Mississippi, and another in the Pacific Ocean. They have no *Sinbad in New Orleans* associations and even their connection with such a title as *New Orleans Sketches* is flimsy enough, being merely that a New Orleans newspaper published them.

[77] Later in an inscription for a gift of his work, probably the longest inscription he ever wrote, Faulkner described almost in amazement his itinerary during those restless weeks while he worked on, and mislaid parts of, *Light in August*. He even included Kingston, Jamaica, among the places where he had worked on the novel, though he is not known ever to have told anyone he had visited that city and investigation there several winters ago produced only a tan.

[78] Joan St. C. Crane, Thomas L. McHaney, and Carl Petersen generously supplied information about manuscripts of *The Wild Palms* recently given to the Alderman Library at the University of Virginia by Mrs. Jill Faulkner Summers.

[79] Discussed at some length in two pieces I have published: "The Pairing of *The Sound and the Fury* and *As I Lay Dying*," *Princeton Library Chronicle* (Faulkner Issue), ed. James B. Meriwether, May, 1957; "Faulkner and Mississippi," in "Faulkner and Yoknapatawpha 1975," *University of Mississippi Studies in English*, Vol. 15, 1978, pp. [139]–159.

[80] *The Wild Palms* has even been called "probably Faulkner's finest novel" by Brian Way, "William Faulkner," *Critical Quarterly*, Spring, 1961, pp. 42–53, according to Carl Petersen, *Each in Its Ordered Place: A Faulkner Collector's Notebook* (Ann Arbor: Ardis Publishers, 1975), p. 248.

[81] (Jackson: University Press of Mississippi, 1975.)

[82] Joseph Blotner, ed., *Selected Letters of William Faulkner*, p. 106.

[83] William Faulkner, *The Wild Palms* (New York: Vintage Books, n.d.) p. 287. Subsequent page references, to this edition, will be given parenthetically in the text.

[84] One writer on Faulkner, committed to proving him a complete misogynist and convinced that he made Charlotte unattractive, calls her "the bony, angular Charlotte Rittenmeyer." In the novel Faulkner describes her "grave simple body a little broader, a little solider than the Hollywood-cod-liver-oil advertisements." (pp. 109–10) When Harry first saw her "he thought she was fat until he saw it was not fat at all but merely that broad, simple profoundly delicate and feminine articulation of Arabian mares." (p. 38)

[85] In *Mosquitoes* Faulkner has Gordon associate "sunburned flame" with Patricia Robyn. The dedication of a copy of his hand-lettered *Marionettes* (1920) in the excellent Faulkner collection at the Humanities Research Center, University of Texas, calls Estelle Franklin's young daughter "A TINY FLOWER OF THE FLAME, THE ETERNAL GESTURE CHRYSTALLIZED [sic]."

[86] Joseph Blotner, *Faulkner: A Biography*, p. 419.

[87] William Rose Benet, ed., *The Reader's Encyclopedia* (New York: Thomas Y. Crowell Co., 1948), p. 884.

[88] Richard Lyons, ed., *Faulkner on Love: A Letter to Marjorie Lyons* (Fargo: The Merrykit Press, 1974) reproduces Faulkner's holograph. This booklet and Joseph Blotner, ed., *Selected Letters of William Faulkner*, p. 301, interpret these holograph words differently, as "That: what he did. Tragic, sad, true; but better than nothing."

[89] G. Wilson Knight, *The Mutual Flame* (London: Methuen, 1962), p. 68.

PERMISSIONS

The permissions gratefully acknowledged here have been essential to the publication of *Helen: A Courtship* and the essay, "Biographical Background for Faulkner's *Helen.*" In addition to granting permissions, many of the people and institutions recorded below have given assistance of many kinds. It is a pleasure to be able to thank:

Jill Faulkner Summers. For permission to publish the text of *Helen: A Courtship* and to quote in "Biographical Background for Faulkner's *Helen*" selected passages from William Faulkner's letters, essays, poetry, and fiction, published and unpublished. For permission to reproduce as an illustration a holograph fragment draft letter by William Faulkner.

William Bell Wisdom. For voluntarily offering permission in the 1950's to arrange the publication someday of *Helen: A Courtship*, as well as *Mayday*, the two Faulkner gift booklets which he had acquired from Helen Baird Lyman. For permission in the 1950's to make photocopies of both booklets. For complete access to his Faulkner collection during two decades before he gave it to Tulane University in 1972. For information and help of every kind in many conversations and in the exchange of more than a hundred and fifty letters. For arranging correspondence with Helen Baird Lyman, and a first interview with her in 1954.

Ann S. Gwyn, Head of the Special Collections Division of The Howard-Tilton Memorial Library at Tulane University, and the *Trustees of Tulane University.* For permission to publish, from The William B. Wisdom Collection of William Faulkner, *Helen: A Courtship*, as well as to use letters by Faulkner to Helen Baird Lyman, photographs, and Mrs. Lyman's portrait of Faulkner, and to draw on "A Memoir—William B. Wisdom, Collector" which Mrs. Gwyn had asked me to contribute to Thomas Bonner, Jr. and Guillermo Náñez Falcon, eds., *William Faulkner: The William B. Wisdom Collection: A Descriptive Catalogue*, New Orleans: The Tulane University Libraries, 1980.

Helen Baird Lyman. For permission to draw on conversations and letters. For information and encouragement in conversations and correspondence. For her generous effort in 1951 to gather additional useful information.

Ann Farnsworth. For permission to quote information concerning her close friend Helen Baird and William Faulkner from conversations and letters, beginning in 1962. For searching out, generously and at considerable trouble, documentation for information. For guidance toward other sources of information and documents.

Meta Wilde. For permission—by a notarized document which in 1968 she generously volunteered should be prepared for her to sign—to quote or use in whatever ways I thought suitable, any information, documents, drawings, and photographs from her relationship with William Faulkner, free from all objections by relatives, friends, and associates. For permission to examine all her letters and other materials from William Faulkner and to make photocopies. For generously, with great expenditure of time and helpful concern, supplying information from her own recollections, and effective guidance to information from others.

Phil Stone and *Emily Whitehurst Stone.* For permission, a decade after the fire, to go through the debris on the site of their burned house, and for help in salvaging a few hundred charred sheets of William Faulkner's early writing, including versions of several of the poems involved in this publication, most of them now in the excellent collections of The Humanities Research Center at the University of Texas and of L. D. Brodsky. For giving permission, immediate and open-handed, to take those salvaged, often severely damaged, sheets from Oxford, Mississippi, to Cambridge, Massachusetts, for professional photocopying before handling could do them additional damage, and to draw on and quote those documents. For hundreds of hours of hospitality and informative conversations over many years beginning in 1948. For guidance to sources of innumerable kinds of information.

Joan Williams. For permission to study and draw on her letters from William Faulkner. For much information and thoughtful judgment, frankly and helpfully given.

Saxe Commins and *Dorothy Berliner Commins.* For permission to read and draw on their correspondence with William Faulkner. For information and help of many kinds.

Lucy S. Howorth. For permission to draw on her written notes of recollections. For helpful conversations and advice.

Ann Green Collins. For permission to use her ideas and research.

The Humanities Research Center, University of Texas. For permission to use the Center's excellent Faulkner collection. For unfailing help of several kinds for several years.

The *Rare Book Department*, and the *Manuscripts Department*, of the *Alderman Library, University of Virginia*, and *Joan St. C. Crane.* For permission to use materials from the Library's excellent Faulkner collections. For quick, effective answers to many questions. For arranging reproduction of the holograph letter fragment used here as an illustration.

The Henry W. and Albert A. Berg Collection, and its Curator *Lola L. Szladits*. For permission to use the Collection's Faulkner documents. For effective assistance of many kinds.

Evans Harrington, Chairman of the Department of English, University of Mississippi. For permission to use passages from my "Faulkner and Mississippi" and "Faulkner: The Man and the Artist" in *The University of Mississippi Studies in English*, University, Mississippi, 1978, Volume 15, lectures given at the University's double sessions of the 1975 annual Faulkner and Yoknapatawpha Conference.

James R. Langford, Director, University of Notre Dame Press. For permission to draw on introductions I supplied for his publication in 1977 of the limited facsimile first-edition of William Faulkner's *Mayday* and in 1978 of its trade edition.

The Johns Hopkins University Press. For permission to quote from David Minter, *William Faulkner: His Life and Work*, 1980.

University Press of Mississippi. For permission to quote from Evans Harrington and Ann Abadie, eds., *The Maker and the Myth*, 1977.

University of Nebraska Press. For permission to quote from Judith Bryant Wittenberg, *Faulkner: The Transfiguration of Biography*, 1979.

Random House. For permission to quote from Joseph Blotner, *Faulkner: A Biography*, 1974; and Joseph Blotner, ed., *Selected Letters of William Faulkner*, 1977.

Yale University Press. For permission to quote from Cleanth Brooks, *William Faulkner: Toward Yoknapatawpha and Beyond*, 1978.

ACKNOWLEDGMENTS

The critical studies to which "Biographical Background for *Helen: A Courtship*" is indebted are acknowledged in the essay and its notes. For information about William Faulkner I am in the debt of many people and institutions who have helped during several years of putting together material for a biographical/critical study and who all will be thanked in detail at a later time. Here practicality and propriety allow acknowledgment of only those directly concerned with this essay centered on a single relationship in William Faulkner's life and work. In alphabetical order, I want here to thank most warmly:

Ann J. Abadie, Richard P. Adams, Conrad Aiken, American Council of Learned Societies, Eleanor Copenhaver Anderson, Elizabeth Prall Anderson, Lucille Antony, Marc Antony, H. Richard Archer,

James R. Baird, Carlos Baker, Hamilton Basso, Robert L. Beare, A. I. Bezzerides, Victoria Fielden Black, Bollingen Foundation, Louise Bonino, William Boozer, Mary Rose Bradford, Dan Brennan, Louis Daniel Brodsky, Calvin S. Brown, Maud Morrow Brown, Nancy Brown, Sallie Falkner Burns, Anthony Buttitta,

Hodding Carter, E. O. Champion, Chatto & Windus, Ltd., Rigmor Christiansen, Alexander P. Clark, Louis Cochran, Jane Coers, Jack Cofield, J. R. Cofield, Marguerite A. Cohn, Maurice E. Coindreau, Memphis *Commercial Appeal*, Dorothy Conkling, Marc Connelly,

Robert W. Daniel, Alfred Dashiell, Myrtle Ramey Demarest, Harold Dempsey, Vincent De Santis, Eric J. Devine, Edith Brown Douds, Caroline Durieux, Howard Duvall, Jr.,

Oxford *Eagle*, Leon Edel, O. B. Emerson, Albert Erskine, James Ezell,

Maud Butler Falkner, Murry C. Falkner, Jr., Robert Farley, Estelle Faulkner, James Murry Faulkner, John W. T. Faulkner, III, William Faulkner, James K. Feibleman, Fidelis Foundation, Flo Field, Victoria Fielden, William Fielden, Louis Andrews Fischer, Shelby Foote, Corey Ford, Ruth Ford, Malcolm A. Franklin, Thomas H. Freeland, III, Julius Friend,

Editions Gallimard, G. M. Gidley, Samuel Louis Gilmore, Evelyn Harter Glick, Morton Goldman, Albert Goldstein, Nina Goolsby, Paul Green, Margery Gumbel,

A. Arthur Halle, Jeffrey Hamm, Dashiell Hammett, Sykes Hartin, Harvard University Library, George W. Healy, Jr., Lillian Hellman, James Hinkle, Mary P. Hirth, Katrina C. Hudson, Branham Hume,

William A. Jackson, Irma Johnson, Nunnally Johnson, Else Jonsson,

Elizabeth M. Kerr, Alfred A. Knopf, Edmund Kohn,

Donelson Lake, Monique Lange, Seymour Lawrence, Rosebud Stone Leatherbury, Harold M. Levy, Library of Congress, Robert Linder, Robert N. Linscott, T. R. Liuzza, Anita Loos, Walt Lowe, Guy C. Lyman, Jr., Margaret Lyman,

John McClure, Joyce Stagg McClure, Thomas L. McHaney, Alabama Falkner McLean, Lillian Friend Marcus, Samuel Marx, Henriette Martin, Martha F. Martin, Massachusetts Institute of Technology Library, F. O. Matthiessen, Louise Meadow, Perry Miller, Arnoldo Mondadori Editore, Harry T. Moore, Phillip E. Mullen,

Constance Nelson, Newberry Library, New Orleans Public Library, New York Public Library, Amy Nyholm,

Dorothy Oldham,

Jo Pagano, Palomar College Library, Michael Papantonio, Dorothy Parker, Peggy Parker, Carl Petersen, Leon Picon, Memphis *Press-Scimitar*, Princeton University Library,

Harry B. Rainold, Walter B. Rideout, Ike Roberts, Warren Roberts,

San Diego State University Library, Joel Sayre, Peter Scott, Margaret T. Silver, James W. Silver, Mrs. Ernest J. Simmons, Robert M. Slabey, Harrison Smith, Ella Somerville, William Spratling, Lawrence Stallings, Lamar Stephens, Myrtle Lewis Stone,

New Orleans *Times-Picayune*, William Towner,

University of California, San Diego, Library, University of Maryland Library, University of Mississippi Library, University of Notre Dame Library, University of Texas Library,

Jean Stein vanden Heuval,

Ben Wasson, James W. Webb, Dean Faulkner Wells, Lawrence Wells, Eudora Welty, Arthur Wilde, Thornton Wilder, Bell I. Wiley, Sallie Murry Williams, Peggy Wilson, Robert Wilson, Tad Wilson,

Yale University Library, Stark Young,

Raymond B. Zeller.

HELEN: A COURTSHIP

TO HELEN, SWIMMING

The gold of smooth and numbered summers does
She back to summer give in swift desire
And hushed the flashing music that is hers
By hands of water mooned to bubbled fire.

Where wind carves of its valleyed unrepose
Hewn changing battlements in slow deploy,
Silver reluctant hands of water lose
Her boy's breast and the plain flanks of a boy.

Throughout this surging city carven yet
To measured ceaseless corridors of seas,
Hands of water hush with green regret
The brown and simple music of her knees.

PASCAGOULA–JUNE–1925

BILL   I

Son of earth was he, and first and last
His heart's whole dream was his, had he been wise,
With space and light to feed it through his eyes,
But with the gift of tongues he was accursed.

Soon he had reft the starlight from the stars
And wind from trees he took, of love and death
He proudly made a sterile shibboleth,
'Till deafened, he forgot what silence was.

Then he found that silence held a Name,
That starlight held a face for him to see,
Found wind once more in grass and leaf, and She
Like silver ceaseless wings that breathe and stir
More grave and true than music, or a flame
Of starlight, and he's quiet, being with her.

PASCAGOULA–JUNE–1925

II

Beneath the apple tree Eve's tortured shape
Glittered in the snake's, her riven breast
Sloped his coils and took the sun's escape
To augur black her sin from east to west.

In winter's night man may keep him warm
Expiating olden sins he did commit;
With fetiches the whip of blood to charm,
Forgetting that, with breath, he's heir to it.

But new gods fall away: the ancient Snake
Is throned and crowned instead and has for minion
That golden apple which will never slake
But feeds and fans man's crumb of fire, when plover
And swallow and shrill northing birds whip over
Nazarene and Roman and Virginian.

PASCAGOULA–JUNE–1925

III

With laggard March, a faun whose stampings ring
And ripple the leaves with hiding: vain pursuit
Of May, anticipated dryad, mute
And yet unwombed of the moist flanks of spring;

Within his green dilemma of faint leaves
His panting puzzled heart is wrung and blind: —
To race the singing corridors of wind,
Retrace waned moons to May for whom he grieves

Or, leafèd close and passionate, to remain
And taste his bitter thumbs 'till May again
Left bare by wild vines' slipping, does incite
To strip the musicked leaves upon her breast
And from a cup unlipped, undreamt, unguessed,
Sip a wine sweetsunned: a god's delight.

PASCAGOULA–JUNE–1925

IV

Her unripe shallow breast is green among
The windy bloom of drunken apple trees
And seven fauns importunate as bees
To sip the thin young honey of her tongue.

The satyr, leafed and hidden, dreams her kiss
His beard amid, leaving his mouth in sight;
Dreams her body in a moony night
Shortening and shuddering into his;

Then sees a faun, bolder than the rest
Slide his hand upon her sudden breast
And feels the life in him go cold and pass
Until the fire their kiss had brought to be
Gutters and faints away: 'tis night, and he
Laughing wrings the bitter wanton grass.

PASCAGOULA–JUNE–1925

PROPOSAL   V

Lets see, I'll say: Between two brief balloons
Of skirts I saw grave chalices of knees
Bloom upward to the cloying cloudy bees
That hive her honeyed hips like little moons.

These slender moons' unsunder I would break;
So soft I'd break that hushed virginity
Of sleep, that in her narrow house would she
Find me drowsing when she came awake.

No: Madam, I love your daughter, I will say.
(From out some leafed dilemma of desire
The wind hales yawning spring, still half undressed,
The hand that once did short to sighs her breast
Slaps her white behind to rosy fire)
. . . Sir, your health, your money: How are they?

PASCAGOULA–JUNE–1925

VI

My health? My health's a fevered loud distress:
Madam, I — Did your knees ever sing
Like hers in passing with such round caress,
And parting, with such sweet reluctance cling?

They must have: you'd not got her otherwise
(How sweet conceiving must have been to you!)
See now the scarce-dreamed curving of her thighs
Beneath that little dress: how grave, how true!

And breasts: can breasts be ever small as these
Twin timorous rabbits' quisitive soft repose?
Can any harped and chorded subtleties
Be half so grave and true as this he knows
Who a tale of olden magic sees
And hears her sheathing music as she goes?

PASCAGOULA–JUNE–1925

VII

The Centaur takes the sun to skull his lyre
That beneath his swept and thunderous hand
Props the sexless curve of sea and land,
Nourishes his ribs of hollow fire.

The Centaur storms, bellied gold with grain
Of all the wild cacaphony of day,
The mare of night in sweet unmarried play
With careful flight is captured once again.

Hail, O Beauty! Helen cries, and she
Would stay the Centaur's rush that there might be
In islanded repose beneath his sweep
A beauty fixed and true, but she forgets
The dream once touched must fade, and that regrets
Buy only one thing sure: undoubtful sleep.

PASCAGOULA–JUNE–1925

VIRGINITY   VIII

Like to the tree that young, reluctant yet
While sap's but troubled rumor of green spring,
Like to the leaf that in warm dark does cling
In maidened sleep unreft, yet passionate;

Or like the cloud that, quicked and shaped for rain
But flees it in a silver hot despair;
The bird that dreams of flight, but does not dare;
The sower loath to sow, and reaps no grain.

Beauty or gold or scarlet, then long sleep:
All this buys brave bright trafficking of breath
That though gray cuckold Time be horned by Death,
Then Death in turn is cuckold, unawake;
But sown cold years the stolen bread you reap
By all the Eves unsistered since the Snake.

MAJORCA–JULY–1925

IX

Goodbye, goodnight: goodnight were more than fair
Since happed I in the losing one, found two,
Gaining in this high and hungry air
Too thin for one, two sisters I must woo.

Alas, my froward one, who would be twain
Yet, willing so, how less you are than either!
What? Husband you with her I wive again?
How sweet a sin, so seeming both, yet neither.

O widowed doubtful bride! No horns he'll feel
Who's pillowed soft and well. And yet, ah me,
If your sleep's simple half did but anneal
Mine own. . . . I'll not share sleep with you, she saith
But come tomorrow: I will give you death.
And leave me cuckold thrice? Goodnight, goodbye.

GENOA–AUGUST–1925

X

Ah no, ah no: my sleep is mine, mine own
And I'll not share it: I'll not make it twain;
This you think you die of, soon is flown:
Leave that be you cant make whole again.

This she told me, thus did speak my pretty
From out the unleafed slightness of her spring,
Her breast unquicked as yet, untrod by pity,
Entranced with single song which she would sing.

But look how does white spring the whole day through
Sing golden-twinned, self-sistered, 'til unfaced
By sun she finds to whom that song was raised,
And there's a marriage made 'tween dusk and dew.
So you no virgin are, my sweet unchaste:
Why, I've lain lonely nights and nights with you.

PAVIA–AUGUST–1925

XI

Let that sleep have no end, which brings me waking
My blanched pillow's womb untwinned, to see
No more this myriad night for whose vain slaking
Night's self is loath, frame this still face to me.

What would I in their lonely paradise
Though deathless golden Helens harp their hair,
Remembering a mouth that sings and sighs
By its own shape in sleep, which is not there?

Let me only wake when long forgot
These thin sweet shoulders bearing yet unbent
The world's whole beauty, leaching, slow assuaged
By this hair's simple twilight, what is not
To all the white that is, though it were blent;
These grave small breasts like sleeping birds uncaged.

PAVIA–AUGUST–1925

XII

Let there be no farewell shaped between
Two mouths that have been one mouth for a day,
Words can break no bonds, while life is green —
Time enough for goodbyes when it's gray.

Life is bony structure, breath is flesh,
Love's the fire to harden and renew;
Farewell's a paper sword, and life in mesh
Laughs the stroke away. And this is true:

The fuelled fire, fecund in her bed,
Contemplative, in close satiety
Shakes not her caverned walls while she is fed;
But once the fuel's eaten up, then she
Screams redly out. And farewell can but be
Of any worth when you and I are dead.

LAGO MAGGIORE–AUGUST–1925

XIII

O I have heard the evening trumpeted
Beneath swept empty skies where hawks had flown
In loneliness of pride 'til each his own
Is wedded with the silence whence has fled

His arrogance with him. O I have seen
That bitter hawk of loneliness and pride
Which was my heart, that swinging curved and died,
Immaculating skies where he had been.

Two hawks there were, but proud and swift with flight
One voided skies with passionate singleness,
And he alone, in stricken ecstasy
Locks beak to beak his shadowed keen distress
In wild and cooling arc of death, and he
Is dead, yet darkly troubled down the night.

LAGO MAGGIORE–AUGUST–1925

XIV

Somewhere is spring with green and simple gold
And cruel April spawned by loined vale,
Somewhere the dying bitter moon grows pale
And day from hill to hill wakes fiery-cold.

In earth yet quicked and filled by wind and sun
Where springs rewomb their vernal gesturing,
Where I now sleep, I closer lie and cling,
But wild were earth housed me at twenty-one.

Somewhere a moon that waxed and found me not
Then waned the windless gardens of the blue,
Somewhere a lost green hurt (but better this
Than in rich desolation long forgot)
Somewhere is youth, a grave sweet mouth to kiss—
Still, you fool, lie still: that's not for you.

PARIS–SEPTEMBER–1925

XV

Knew I love once? Was it love or grief
This young body by where I had lain?
And my heart, this single stubborn leaf
That will not die, though root and branch be slain?

O mother Sleep, when one by one these years
Bell their bitter note, and die away
Down Time's slow evening, passionless as tears
When sorrow long has ebbed and grief is gray;

Though warm in dark between the breasts of Death,
That other breast forgot where I did lie,
And from the stalk are stripped the leaves of breath,
There's yet one stubborn leaf that will not die
But restless in the wild and bitter earth,
Gains with each dawn a death, with dusk a birth.

PARIS–SEPTEMBER–1925

A NOTE ON THE TEXT

The limited first edition of *Helen: A Courtship* published this year by The Friends of the Tulane University Library and the Yoknapatawpha Press of Oxford, Mississippi, reproduced in facsimile William Faulkner's gift book with its hand lettering. This trade edition set in type follows the author's original spelling, capitalization, and punctuation except in five places, where changes have been made to avoid confusion for the reader: In line 3 of VI, Faulkner's apostrophe has been removed from "her's." In line 4 of XII, "its" has been changed to "it's." In lines 10 and 13 of V, lines 6 and 7 of VI and lines 11 and 12 of XIV, Faulkner's brackets have been changed to parentheses to avoid the confusing implication that words have been added editorially; Faulkner himself made the same change to parentheses in other versions of the poems.

Faulkner's hand-lettered reversals of s, S, N, and J, as well as his using V for U, have been normalized in the type of this edition.

Mississippi Poems

INTRODUCTION
by
Joseph Blotner

When Myrtle Ramey and her classmates entered the Third Grade of the Oxford Graded School in September of 1906, they were joined by a new boy who had done so well in Miss Annie Chandler's First Grade class that Principal R. L. Harris had decided he should skip Second Grade. William Cuthbert Falkner was a quiet boy who generally kept more to himself than others, but he took to Myrtle Ramey. She attended school less than half of each day, for she was delicate and still suffering the after effects of scarlet fever; but she was intelligent, sensitive, and firm-minded. It did not take her long to realize that her new classmate was talented as well as sympathetic. Turning nine late that September, he continued to earn from Miss Laura Eades the same grades of Perfect and Excellent that he had earned from Miss Annie Chandler. He was also artistic. He drew pictures in his textbooks, and when he completed an assignment of making a cube out of paper, his work was perfect whereas Myrtle's efforts had reduced her to weeping frustration.[1]

The two students moved up together through the succeeding grades, and by the time they were in the Seventh, Billy Falkner would show her not only his sketches but also stories and poems which they sometimes illustrated. He was reading a good deal of poetry and writing out the lines of other poets as well as his own. In elaborate calligraphy he copied out sensuous verses from *The Song of Solomon*, though his own images tended more towards those of the Greek pastoral mode. In his reading of prose he ranged far afield. That summer, when the Rameys and the Falkners went to the nearby resort of Lafayette Springs, the two friends would stretch out in barrel-stave hammocks strung between oak trees. Sometimes they would pull each other with the cords attached to each hammock. At other times they took turns reading *The Arkansas Traveler* aloud.[2] Billy was the leader in this and proceeded to *The Pilgrim's Progress*, though he soon found himself unable to interest Myrtle in it. Her mentor in other areas as well, he provided her first cigarette, rolling rabbit tobacco in paper torn from a Sears, Roebuck catalogue.

By the time they were Eleventh Graders, he was bored with the academic side of school. Often a truant, he attended principally for sports and other occasional extra-curricular activities such as the planning of the Eleventh Grade yearbook. (There was then no Twelfth Grade.) He did a number of pen and ink sketches for it, most of them comic with appropriate captions for the classroom scenes but a few of them embodying the familiar high school refrains of appreciation of learning and idealistic dedication of the future. The project did not go beyond the planning stage, and it was probably at this time that he gave these sketches to Myrtle Ramey, the first of a number of such gifts. She pasted the sketches in her grade school scrapbook.[3]

William Faulkner would continue to enjoy sketching for its own sake, but his creative energies were being absorbed in much more serious work. By now he had come to know Phil Stone—four years older, brilliant, and as academically oriented as Billy Falkner was not. A lawyer-to-be, trained at the University of Mississippi and Yale, he had quickly discerned in the work of this son of family friends what were to him unmistakable signs of real talent.

Now, and for more than a decade to come, Stone would

take upon himself the role of mentor, encourager, and promoter—pressing on his younger friend the books of poetry and criticism he brought back from Yale or, once again resident in Oxford, the books he ordered from his favorite store in New Haven. Joining the family law practice, he would also supply Falkner with the secretarial services of the office as well as his own as a combination press agent and patron of sorts.

In the next decade, Myrtle Ramey would continue to see William Falkner occasionally, at the homes of friends and at dances, on the Square or at the Depot. He continued his practice of giving her gifts. One, which may date from about 1916, was a signed pen and ink sketch of a young man and woman dancing, a precursor of a number of drawings in much the same style that he would later contribute to *Ole Miss* yearbooks at the University of Mississippi.[4] Sometimes when Myrtle saw him he would be sporting a cane and spats. Sometimes he would be dressed like a bum. Much had intervened as his life followed an unpredictable pattern.

He had worked briefly in the bank of which his grandfather was president but soon left that job to become a footloose roamer. After wartime training with the RAF in Canada he had returned home, at liberty again for months until he spent an irregular year and a half as a special student at the University of Mississippi. He went to New York briefly as a clerk in a bookstore. Returning home once more he put in nearly three years as an unhappy and maladroit campus postmaster before he was forced to resign. He did so with relief and a feeling of deliverance.

As the year of 1924 drew to a close, his first book appeared, his name on it now spelled William Faulkner. It was the cycle of nineteen pastoral poems entitled *The Marble Faun*, with a preface by Phil Stone. Faulkner was now preparing for a new phase of his life, planning to go abroad, to live and work in

Phil Stone's law office

Europe, where perhaps his first substantial recognition might come as it had come to other American artists such as Robert Frost and Ernest Hemingway.

On the day before New Year's Eve, Phil Stone asked Myrtle Ramey to come to his office for tea. "Getting very British, aren't we," she responded, quick and insouciant as ever. But she was there on time, to find Faulkner there too. Before she left Stone's office that afternoon her onetime grade school classmate had presented her with an inscribed copy of *The Marble Faun*. "To Myrtle Ramey," he had written, "my old friend and school mate. / Bill Faulkner." Phil Stone wrote, "A greeting to my old friend Myrtle Ramey" and added his signature. The poet on that afternoon also gave her something rarer: a sheaf of onionskin sheets bearing copies of twelve poems, each of them autographed. Faulkner would put together several such small gift volumes, sometimes binding them carefully. But no other would have the elaborate reservation of rights in Phil Stone's hand. Work of Faulkner's had been sent to editors and publishers from Stone's office before. Some of these poems might have already been offered for publication. If there should be an acceptance while Faulkner was in Europe, Stone would act for him as his agent. Faulkner also gave her a seven-page carbon typescript of one of his ventures as a literary essayist: "Verse, Old and Nascent: A Pilgrimage," which would be published in the New Orleans magazine, *The Double Dealer*, the following April.[5]

The essay was different from two others on poetry he had written earlier. The first of these was a review of William Alexander Percy's *In April Once*. It had appeared in the university newspaper, *The Mississippian*, on November 10, 1920. In it he had written that Percy, "like alas! how many of us," had been born out of his time, that he had an affinity for Swinburne and a fear of "the dark of modernity. . . ." Faulkner ended with a qualified judgment. Percy's book had music in it, but he was "a violinist with an inferior instrument. . . ."

Nonetheless, Faulkner concluded that "the gold outweighs the dross."[6] Three months later, on February 16, 1921, in *The Mississippian* once again, he gave unqualified praise to Conrad Aiken's *Turns and Movies*. "In the fog generated by the mental puberty of contemporary American versifiers while writing inferior Keats or sobbing over the middle west," he wrote, "appears one rift of heaven sent blue—the poems of Conrad Aiken." He praised Aiken's "experiments with an abstract three dimensional verse patterned on polyphonic music form," but he also liked the elements that suggested the Greeks, the French Symbolists, and John Masefield. He speculated that in fifteen years, "when the tide of aesthetic sterility which is slowly engulfing us has withdrawn, our first great poet will be left." Aiken, he thought, might be the man.[7]

"Verse, Old and Nascent" was different from these two pieces in that it was a general essay rather than a review and was even more a personal statement. It had to be read with caution, for here as elsewhere in Faulkner's writing and his life, he was adopting a persona, a screen for his innermost self. The poetic ardor of the earlier writings had been replaced by a rather cynical and world-weary tone, as when he confessed to first reading and employing verse "for the purpose of furthering various philanderings in which I was engaged, secondly, to complete a youthful gesture I was then making, of being 'different' in a small town. Later, my interest in fornication waning, I turned inevitably to verse, finding therein an emotional counterpart far more satisfactory...." (In *The Double Dealer* "my interest in fornication" was toned down to "my concupiscence.") But even granting that Faulkner here adopted the pose of the blasé sophisticate, one could still find insights into his poetic preferences from his middle teens to his later twenties.

Faulkner had dated *The Marble Faun* "April, May, June, 1919." Poetry which he composed subsequently showed how many influences he had assimilated. This was also true of the poems he gave to Myrtle Ramey, and much of their interest for the admirer of his work lies in the way in which they look not only backward but forward, anticipating themes and figures to come in his fiction. But he did not repudiate this early work. He would think well enough of it to publish eight of these poems in his only other book of verse, *A Green Bough*, which appeared in 1933, when he had already published three of his masterworks in prose.[8] Throughout his life he would conceive of poetry in the most exalted terms, defining it, a third of a century after *The Marble Faun*, as "some moving, passionate moment of the human condition distilled to its absolute essence." Looking back over that time span he would say, "I believe that any writer wants first to be a poet. When he finds that he can't write first-rate poetry—and poetry of all must be first-rate—there are no degrees of it . . . then he tries short stories, which is the next severe medium. When that fails, he goes to the novel. That is, he wants first to take the tragedy and passion of experience, life, and put it into fourteen words. If he can't, he tries two thousand words. If he fails that then he takes a hundred thousand."

Of the twelve poems which Faulkner had given Myrtle, six were dated. Versions of two of the others which Faulkner retained were also dated, all eight within the last three months of 1924. The fact that he had written on his essay, "Verse, Old and Nascent," the date "October, 1924" suggests strongly that the sentiments he had expressed in it would be reflected in the poems. Despite the imitations of T. S. Eliot and e. e. cummings in both published and unpublished verse, these sentiments were strongly anti-modernist. His recital of the history of his poetic preference told why, tracing his path from Swinburne to membership in "the pack belling loudly after contemporary poets" and then to Housman, he went to Shakespeare, Spenser, the Elizabethans, Shelley and Keats, finding the work of the last two so moving that he longed to hear voices like theirs in his own time. One work he mentioned would sound more resonantly in his own writing than any other single poem: Keats' "Ode on a Grecian Urn."

Of all the poets he mentioned in the essay, the one most often echoed in the gift poems is A. E. Housman. But there is not the uniformity of tone in *Mississippi Poems* that was produced in *The Marble Faun* by the themes of stasis and loss and the pastoral imagery. The Roman numerals of the first seven poems suggested a progression. There was an incomplete one of sorts, extending to the unnumbered poems, too, in the use of months and, to a lesser extent, the seasons. The treatment of landscape, of the earth, of sun, moon, and stars, also provided a certain consistency. Behind the treatment of the particular and immediate were references to the general and permanent, emphasized by the poet's use in poem VII of the hills and trees which were there before he lived and would shelter him after death. The unnumbered poems represented varied concerns and subjects, some of them suggesting links with other work. All of the poems were suffused with the romanticism which marked Faulkner's early work, a romanticism whose most persistent characteristic was a melancholy often deepening into bitter pessimism. Rather than seeking the kind of unity that governed some of Faulkner's other gift books, however, it is probably best briefly to glance at each poem separately in turn in this collection derived from a lasting friendship rather than a passionate attachment.

Faulkner retained a copy of poem I dated October 18, 1924, but the archaic words and the accented syllable in the third stanza and the Grecian reference in the fourth suggest that this may have been a reworking of a much earlier poem. Like this poem's references to sorrow, the references in poem II to youth and despair, to heartbreak and death, suggest the response to Housman which Faulkner had made so wholeheartedly in the essay. This is one of the three poems being published here for the first time.

Although poem III closed on a note of sorrow, it moved

Phil Stone

through all four seasons, and the poet could tell his reader to rejoice that the spring would come again. A version which Stone kept was dated September 10, 1924. This subject and the imagery Faulkner employed to treat it continued to engage him. Using the courtesan for his central image, he composed a Petrarchan sonnet, never published, which he entitled "New Orleans." He used a kind of prose equivalent in the last portion of an eleven-part sketch published under the title "New Orleans" in *The Double Dealer* for January–February of 1925. Much of the same imagery appeared early in the Prologue of his second novel, *Mosquitos*, which was set in New Orleans and published in 1927. The prose piece "New Orleans" was reprinted in a collection called *Salmagundi* in 1932, and a year later poem III of the present volume would be poem XXXV in *A Green Bough*. Something of the same use of the four seasons, juxtaposed to the presence of death, reappeared in a story called "Sepulture South: Gaslight," which came out in *Harper's Bazaar* thirty years to the month after his gift to Myrtle Ramey.

Set in November, poem IV was also dominated by one central image, the wild geese whose lonely cry prompted the poet's melancholy feelings of frustration and isolation. The second and third stanzas echoed the sense of a poem from *A Shropshire Lad* that Faulkner knew by heart, poem XLVIII, where the poet enjoined himself, "Be still, be still, my soul. . . ." Faulkner would put it even more plainly in an unpublished sonnet entitled "Admonishes His Heart" and dated "14 march 1927," in which the words were even closer to Housman's. Then, a year later, when he was writing *The Sound and the Fury*, he would present Quentin Compson's recollection of the same sentiments as he heard them from his father. His use of the geese as a symbol for loneliness would find its most powerful expression in the interior monologue of Addie Bundren in *As I Lay Dying*, where she would recall the flight of the wild geese, in words very close to those of this poem, not once but twice. It became poem XXVIII in *A Green Bough*. A week before the book appeared the poem was published as "Over the World's Rim" in *The New Republic* for April 12, 1933.

Poem V, the only happy one in the group, was also notable for the way Faulkner was delineating in poetry the sort of bucolic figure he had rendered in prose two years before in a sketch called "The Hill," which appeared in *The Mississippian*. With this kind of figure and landscape, despite the diction which still echoed the late romantic verse he would soon discard, he was moving closer to the people and the scenes of Yoknapatawpha County. It became poem VIII of *A Green Bough*, where IX began with a plowman slowly homeward wending and X gave a paraphrase of the last part of "The Hill."

In the sixth poem, previously unpublished, and the seventh poem the poet employed diction and sounded laments Housman might have used. A copy of VII which Phil Stone retained was dated October 16, and two which Faulkner kept were dated a day later. This was apparently a poem Faulkner labored over a good deal. The typescript title of the two copies dated earlier included "Mississippi Hills," though when Faulkner used it as poem XLIV to conclude *A Green Bough*, he deleted the title altogether as well as eliminating the first and last quatrains and rewriting the first two lines of the second quatrain and the first of the third. With a few minor variants the poem appeared earlier as "My Epitaph" in an issue of *Contempo* devoted to Faulkner's work which was published on February 1, 1932. That same year it was published in *An Anthology of the Younger Poets* and in a revised version by itself as *This Earth*. In 1934 it appeared in *Mississippi Verse* under the title "If There Be Grief." Its placement in *A Green Bough* would indicate the valuation Faulkner placed on the poem, and it would be his most moving to many readers. As Cleanth Brooks has observed, however, the thought it embodied received an even more moving statement in his prose: Ike McCaslin's perception of the life in death that both Lion and Sam Fathers achieved in "The Bear," the noblest of the seven segments that made up *Go Down, Moses* of 1942.[9]

Though placed eighth in the order of the poems, the next one bore the latest date of composition, "December 15, 1924." Despite its title, "March" dealt with epochs rather than just one month. In its glancing at Eve and Christ, at Roman and Virginian, the poem suggested the work of that poet Faulkner came to admire later: William Butler Yeats, but the predominant tone and diction again pointed to the influence of Housman. Faulkner's last line called to mind the last stanza of poem XXXI of *A Shropshire Lad*, which began, "On Wenlock Edge the wood's in trouble. . . ." In June of 1925 this sonnet would become a part of *To Helen: A Courtship*, another gift booklet, presented to a young woman for whom Faulkner had cared deeply. Her name was Helen Baird, and he would dedicate *Mosquitos* to her.[10] He would use the poem as XLII in *A Green Bough*, and the dominant image would survive as a reference to "Eve and the snake" thirty years later in *A Fable*, signifying to Lewis P. Simpson, Faulkner's recognition of the conquest of the historicism of the Hebraic-Christian interpretation of sexuality over the cosmic sexuality of the Greco-Roman garden.[11]

"The Gallows" was another poem in which Faulkner seemed to be using his own equivalent of Housman's modified Shropshire dialect. Adding three quatrains which recalled specifically Housman's gallows poems—IX, XLVII, and perhaps something of XXXII, all in *A Shropshire Lad*—Faulkner made "The Gallows" poem XIV of *A Green Bough*. There it was preceded by three poems and followed by one more which were even more clearly indebted to the man who, Faulkner had written in "Verse, Old and Nascent," had found the secret which the moderns were vainly seeking.

Faulkner wrote "Pregnancy" (converted by an uncorrected

Myrtle Ramey

typographical error to the "Pregnacy" which we see here) in a very different idiom, and though the winter setting, with the promise of spring at the end, linked the poem to the others emphasizing months and seasons, it would suggest to a reader familiar with Faulkner's early verse a poem that might fit into a very different context. "Pregnancy" would lose its title and become XXIX in *A Green Bough*. The long second poem of that volume had in one draft been called "Marriage." It was part of a gift volume Faulkner had made for Estelle Franklin, who had broken their unofficial engagement to marry another man three years before, but who would finally marry Faulkner in 1929. "Marriage" was full of tension and animosity rather than bliss, and one can only speculate about the extent to which it had a special meaning, either for Faulkner or Estelle Franklin. Pregnancy seemed to produce as little happiness here as marriage had in the earlier poem. (Poem III in *A Green Bough* was also set in a cave and employed star imagery, but there were few other resemblances, and in one draft Faulkner had entitled this poem "Floyd Collins," in reference to the well-publicized entrapment and death of Collins in a Kentucky cave in 1925.) The most striking use of the girl's situation and some of the phrases used to describe it would come half a dozen years later in *As I Lay Dying* when Dewey Dell, unhappily pregnant, would say she felt like "a wet seed wild in the hot blind earth."

The Marble Faun had been structured around the cycle of the year, and though "March," the eighth in *Mississippi Poems*, bore the latest composition date, Faulkner moved to the last months of the year with the sequence of poems which brought this gift volume to an end. The last two were linked by the pervasive sense of loss and by the inability of the idea of the inevitable return of spring to mitigate the cold within the heart and the earth. Both the title and date of the first of these two poems suggested a wider frame of reference which Phil Stone made explicit when he sent it to *The Atlantic*

William Faulkner

Monthly on November 13 describing it as "An Armistice Day Poem." Despite this topical reference to The First World War, the poem suggested Swinburne and Edward Fitzgerald's *The Rubáiyát of Omar Khayyám* more than the poets of the recent war. Though *The Atlantic* did not buy the poem, Faulkner showed his fondness for it by using the last quatrain—titled "Soldier"—as the epigraph for *Soldiers' Pay*. He would use it again as poem XXX in *A Green Bough*, which appeared a week after the poem had been published in *The New Republic* on April 12, 1933. The last quatrain of "December: To Elise" sounded much like the poems of lamentation that had been prompted by his one-sided love affair with Helen Baird. He did not include it in *A Green Bough*, and it remained unpublished until its appearance in this facsimile edition. He retained a copy of another version of this poem which he had dated five days earlier. But this version did not include the word "December" in the title, suggesting that perhaps Faulkner had added it to help round out the little cycle of poems he had given to Myrtle Ramey.

Nearly a year before *Mosquitos* appeared, Myrtle Ramey had married a young man named Frederick Van B. Demarest. She was another of the old gang who had married while Faulkner, with at least two unhappy love affairs behind him, remained single as he approached his thirtieth birthday. The melancholy of the poems he had given her would remain in many ways an essential part of his personality. For years to come he would inscribe copies of his novels to her as they appeared—always in her maiden name, never her married one. And on the occasions when he would see her during her brief visits home each year, the old comradeship which had begun between the quiet boy and the delicate girl in Miss Laura Eades' Third Grade class would still be there. As time had gone on he had grown more quiet, if anything, while she had become more assertive, more sure of herself, as she had begun to be by the time they had read and fished and swum together that summer at Lafayette Springs.

On one of these visits in the early Nineteen-Thirties, she went out to the golf course. Her party heard the cry of "Fore," and when the other group played through she saw that Faulkner was part of it. Looking straight ahead, he did not notice her.

"Hi, William," she said.

"Why, Myrtle Ramey," he answered.

"Next time you go by without seeing me," she told him, "I'm going to kick you in the shins."

He smiled. "Same old Moitle," he said.

She kept the gift of *Mississippi Poems* and the essay and the drawings for more than half a century, until they were acquired by Faulkner collector and student Louis Daniel Brodsky, who has generously made his collection available in several ways to those who treasure Faulkner's work. It is a particular pleasure to acknowledge the debt owed by all those readers to Jill Faulkner Summers for giving her consent to the publication of the poems—especially the three which appear here for the first time—and to Myrtle Ramey and Louis Daniel Brodsky. Finally, this book itself is an act of homage acknowledging the debt of his readers to the artist himself, whose work promises to achieve the immortality alluded to in many different moods and modes in *Mississippi Poems*.

Joseph Blotner

NOTES

1. For additional treatment of the material in this introduction see Joseph Blotner, *Faulkner: A Biography*, New York: Random House, 1974.
2. Professor Louis D. Rubin, Jr., recalls the popularity of joke books in the early years of this century. They were easily available in the South, for "every railroad station used to have a rack full of joke books." LDR to JB, 24 Jan. 1979. Professor John Seelye has called my attention to an entry in the *National Union Catalog Pre-1956 Imprints* which appears to be a reprint of the book William Falkner and Myrtle Ramey enjoyed: "*The Arkansas Traveler/* Jokes, monologues, funny anecdotes, flashes of wit, original cartoons selected from the Arkansas Traveler. Introducing the quaint wisdom of Opie Read. Chicago, Stein Publishing House, c1945." JS to JB, 25 Jan. 1979.
3. For this information I am indebted to Louis Daniel Brodsky. LDB to JB, 22 Jan. 1979.
4. Faulkner's friend, Ben Wasson, dates this drawing at about 1916. LDB to JB, 22 Jan. 1979.
5. The essay was reprinted in *William Faulkner: Early Prose and Poetry*, edited by Carvel Collins, Boston: Little, Brown and Company, 1962, where "The Hill," referred to below, was also reprinted.
6. *Ibid.*, p. 73.
7. *Ibid.*, pp. 74–76.
8. For a valuable survey of Faulkner's poetry see Keen Butterworth, "A Census of Manuscripts and Typescripts of William Faulkner's Poetry," in *A Faulkner Miscellany*, edited by James B. Meriwether, Jackson: University Press of Mississippi, 1974, pp. 70–97.
9. Cleanth Brooks, *Toward Yoknapatawpha and Beyond*, New Haven: Yale University Press, 1978, pp. 20–21.
10. *Ibid.*, pp. 52, 54–60.
11. Lewis P. Simpson, "Sex and History: Origins of Faulkner's Apocrypha," in *The Maker and the Myth: Faulkner and Yoknapatawpha, 1977*, edited by Evans Harrington and Ann J. Abadie, Jackson: University Press of Mississippi, 1978, p. 46.

MISSISSIPPI POEMS

I.

Shall I recall this tree, when I am old,
This hill, or how this valley fills with sun
And green afternoon is bought for morning's gold
And sold again for sleep when day is done?

As well to ask the wine to say what grapes
Distilled their purple suns when full and hot,
Or me what body hands' remembering shapes
To trouble heart when mind has long forgot.

The hushèd wings of wind are feathered high
And shape the tree-tops, vaguely fugitive,
To shake my heart with hill and vale for aye
When vale and hill itself no longer live.

But let me take this silver-minted moon
And bridle me the wind centaurs that whirled
Out of Hellas, grained at beauty's noon,
And ride the cold old sorrow of the world.

II.

Moon of death, moon of bright despair:
Deep in a silver sea the earth is drowned
And the trees her dead and restless hair
Seeking the surface like a troubled sound.

How oft to this despair must I awake
To feel a bleeding wound within my side
As though with Time I had exchanged, to take
His own cold place where He is crucified.

Shall Time lie here, where I was young and lay
This body by for bright heart's ravishment,
Craved in these thighs where I sought death for aye?
Shall Time suck dry the mouth where mine was blent?

Time, the heir to all, might leave me this
Since the heart-break is so soon forgot:
O mother earth, be kind: who gave us bliss
Can give a night where moon and bird are not.

III.

INDIAN SUMMER.

The courtesan is dead, for all her subtle ways,
Her bonds are loosed in brittle and bitter leaves,
Her last long backward look's to see who grieves
The imminent night toward her reverted gaze.

Another will reign supreme, now she is dead
And winter's lean clean rain sweeps out her room,
For man's delight and anguish: with old new bloom
Crowning his desire, garlanding his head.

So, too, the world, turning to cold and death
When swallows empty the blue and drowsy days
And clean rain scatters the ghost of Summer's breath—
The courtesan that's dead, for all her subtle ways—

Spring will come! Rejoice! But still is there
An old sorrow sharp as wood-smoke on the air.

IV.

WILD GEESE.

Over the world's rim, drawing bland November
Reluctant behind them, drawing the moons of cold;
What their lonely voices stir to remember
This dust ere it was flesh? what restless old

Dream a thousand years was safely sleeping,
Wakes my blood to sharp unease? what horn
Rings out to them? Was I free once, sweeping
Their wild and lonely skies ere I was born?

This hand that shaped my body, that gave me vision,
Made me a slave to clay for a fee of breath.
Sweep on, O wild and lonely! Mine the derision,
Thine the splendor and speed, the cleanness, of death.

Over the world's rim, out of some splendid noon,
Seeking some high desire, and not in vain!
They fill and empty the red and dying moon
And crying, cross the rim of the world again.

V.

He furrows the brown earth, doubly sweet
To a hushed great passage of wind
Dragging its shadow. Beneath his feet
The furrow breaks, and at its end

He turns. With peace about his head
Traverses he again the earth: his own,
Still with enormous promises of bread
And clean its odorous strength about him blown.

From the shimmering azure of the wood
A blackbird whistles, cool and mellow;
And here, where for a space he stood
To fill his lungs, a spurting yellow

Rabbit bursts, its hurtling gold
Muscled to erratic lines
Of fluid fear across the mold.
He shouts. The darkly liquid pines

Mirror his falling voice as leaf
Raises clear cool depths to meet its falling self;
And then again the blackbird, thief
Of silence in a glossy pelf,

Inscribes the answer to its life
Upon the white page of the sky:
The furious emptiness of strife
For him to read who passes by.

He moves again, to bells of sheep
Slow as clouds on hills of green;
Somewhere rumorous waters sleep
Beyond a faint-leaved willow screen.

Wind and sun and sleep: he can
Furrow the brown earth, doubly sweet
To a simple heart, for here a man
Might bread him with his hands and feet.

VI.

THE POET GOES BLIND.

You, who so soon with night would break
My day in half, before it reached its noon:
What sport is this— the sleeper to awake
Into a day he sought not, then to take
His waking span and rieve its sun and moon?

Three score and ten were short enough for learning—
Before the dark descends for aye on me—
These streams and hills, so give me time for burning
Upon my heart their eve- and dawnward-turning
Past all forgetting, if I must not see.

The wind blows from the world, upon my cheek,
Molding unseen hills, and I despair.
You are strong: there's hate and fear to wreak
Your might upon! O leave me eyes to seek,
To wing my heart through golden-chambered air.

You, who to leaf and bud and tree,
Raised me from dust and crimson roots of pain,
Take not mine eyes! take limbs; let me be
Tongueless, dead to sound: take breath from me
Or give me back my golden world again.

VII.

MISSISSIPPI HILLS: MY EPITAPH.

Far blue hills, where I have pleasured me,
Where on silver feet in dogwood cover
Spring follows, singing close the bluebird's "Lover!"
When to the road I trod an end I see.

Let this soft mouth, shapèd to the rain,
Be but golden grief for grieving's sake,
And these green woods be dreaming here to wake
Within my heart when I return again.

Return I will! Where is there the death
While in these blue hills slumbrous overhead
I'm rooted like a tree? Though I be dead,
This soil that holds me fast will find me breath.

The stricken tree has no young green to weep
The golden years we spend to buy regret.
So let this be my doom, if I forget
That there's still spring to shake and break my sleep.

DECEMBER:
TO ELISE.

Where has flown the spring we knew together?
Barren are the boughs of yesteryear;
But I have seen your hands take wintry weather
And smoothe the rain from it, and leave it fair.

If from sleep's tree these brown and sorry leaves,
If but regret could drown when springs depart,
No more would be each day that drips and grieves
A bare and bitter year within my heart.

In my heart's winter you were budding tree,
And spring seemed all the sweeter, being late;
You the wind that brought the spring to be
Within a garden that was desolate.

You were all the spring, and May and June
Greened brighter in your flesh, but now is dull
The year with rain, and dead the sun and moon,
And all the world is dark, O beautiful.

MARCH

Beneath the apple tree Eve's tortured shape
Glittered in the snake's, her riven breast
Sloped his coils and took the sun's escape
To augur black her sin from east to west.

Through winter's night man can take for warm
Forgiveness of old sins he did commit,
With fetiches the ship of blood to charm,
Forgetting that, with birth, he's heir to it.

But old gods fall away— the ancient Snake
Is throned and crowned instead, who has for minion
That golden apple which will never slake
But feeds and fans man's crumb of fire— when plover
And eagle and shrill northing birds whip over
Nazarine and Roman and Virginian.

NOVEMBER 11TH

Gray the day, and all the year is cold,
Across the empty land the swallows' cry
Marks the south-flown spring: naught is bowled
Save winter, in the sky.

O sorry earth, when this bleak bitter sleep
Stirs and turns, and time once more is green,
In empty path and lane grass will creep,
With none to tread it clean.

April and May and June, and all the dearth
Of heart to green it for, to hurt and wake;
What good is budding, gray November earth,
No need to break your sleep for greening's sake.

The hushed plaint of wind in stricken trees
Shivers the grass in path and lane
And Grief and Time are tideless golden seas—
Hush, hush! he's home again.

THE GALLOWS.

His mother said: I'll make him
A lad as ne'er has been
(And rocked him closely, stroking
His soft hair's golden sheen)
His bright youth will be metal
No alchemist has seen.

His mother said: I'll give him
A bright and high desire
'Till all the dross of living
Burns clean within his fire.
He'll be strong and merry
And he'll be clean and brave,
And all the world will rue it
When he is dark in grave.

But dark will treat him kinder
Than man would anywhere
(With barren winds to rock him
—Though now he doesn't care—
And hushed and haughty starlight
To stroke his golden hair)

PREGNACY

As to an ancient music's hidden fall
Her seed in the huddled dark was warm and wet,
And three cold stars were riven in the wall:
Rain and fire and death above her door were set.

Her hands moaned on her breast in blind and supple fire,
Made light within her cave: she saw her harried
Body wrung to a strange and bitter lyre,
Whose music once was pure strings simply married.

One to another in sleepy diffidence
Her thin and happy sorrows once were wed,
And what tomorrow's chords be recompense
For yesterday's single song unravishèd?

Three stars in her heart when she awakes
As winter's sleep breaks greening in the rain,
And in the caverned earth spring's rumor shakes,
As in her loins, the tilled and quickened grain.

VERSE, OLD AND NASCENT:
A PILGRIMAGE

At the age of sixteen, I discovered Swinburne. Or rather, Swinburne discovered me, springing from some tortured undergrowth of my adolescence, like a highwayman, making me his slave. My mental life at that period was so completely and smoothly veneered with surface insincerity— obviously necessary to me at that time, to support intact my personal integrity— that I can not tell to this day exactly to what depth he stirred me, just how deeply the foot-prints of his passage are left in my mind. It seems to me now that I found him nothing but a flexible vessel into which I might put my own vague emotional shapes without breaking them. It was years later that I found in him much more than bright and bitter sound, more than a satisfying tinsel of blood and death and gold and the inevitable sea. True, I dipped into Shelley and Keats— who doesn't, at that age?— but they did not move me.

I do not think it was assurance so much, merely complacence and a youthful morbidity, which counteracted them and left me cold. I was not interested in verse for verse's sake then. I read and employed verse, firstly, for the purpose of furthering various philanderings in which I was engaged, secondly, to complete a youthful gesture I was then making, of being "different" in a small town. Later, my interest in fornication waning, I turned inevitably to verse, finding therein an emotional conterpart far more satisfactory for two reasons: (1) No partner was required (2) It was so much simpler just to close a book, and take a walk. I do not mean by this that I ever found anything sexual in Swinburne: there is no sex in Swinburne. The mathematician, surely; and eroticism just as there is eroticism in form and color and movement wherever found. But not that tortured sex in—say—D. H. Lawrence.

It is a time-honored custom to read Omar to one's mistress as an accompanyment to consummation—a sort of stringèd obbligate among the sighs. I found that verse could be employed not only to temporarily blind the spirit to the ungraceful posturings of the flesh, but also to speed onward the whole affair. Ah, women, with their hungry snatching little souls! With a man it is—quite often— art for art's sake; with a woman it is always art for the artist's sake.

Whatever it was that I found in Swinburne, it completely satisfied me and filled my inner life. I cannot understand now how I could have regarded the others with such dull complacency. Surely, if one be moved at all by Swinburne he must inevitably find in Swinburne's forerunners some kinship. Perhaps it is that Swinburne, having taken his heritage and elaborated it to the despair of any would-be poet, has coarsened it to tickle the dullest of palates as well as the most discriminating, as used water can be drunk by both hogs and gods.

Therefore, I believe I came as near as possible to approaching poetry with an unprejudiced mind. I was subject to the usual proselyting of an older person, but the strings were pulled so casually as scarcely to influence my point of view. I had no opinions at that time, the opinions I later formed were all factitious and were discarded. I approached Poetry unawed, as if to say; "Now, let's see what you have." Having used verse, I would now allow verse to use me if it could.

When the co-ordinated chaos of the war was replaced by the unco-ordinated chaos of peace I took seriously to reading verse. With no background whatever I joined the pack belling loudly after contemporary poets. I could not always tell what it was all about but "This is the stuff," I told myself, believing, like so many, that if one cried loudly enough to be heard above the din, and so convinced others that one was "in the know," one would be automatically accoladed. I joined an emotional B.P.O.E.

The beauty— spiritual and physical— of the South lies in the fact that God has done so much for it and man so little. I have this for which to thank whatever gods may be: that having fixed my roots in this soil all contact, saving by the printed word, with contemporary poets is impossible.

That page is closed to me forever. I read Robison and Frost with pleasure, and Aldington; Conrad Aiken's minor music still echoes in my heart; but beyond these, that period might have never been. I no longer try to read the others at all.

It was "The Shropshire Lad" which closed the period. I found a paper-bound copy in a bookshop and when I opened it I discovered there the secret after which the moderns course howling like curs on a cold trail in a dark wood, giving off, it is true, an occasional note clear with beauty, but curs just the same. Here was reason for being born into a fantastic world: discovering the splendor of fortitude, the beauty of being of the soil like a tree about which fools might howl and which winds of disillusion and death and despair might strip, leaving it bleak, without bitterness; beautiful in sadness.

From this point the road is obvious. Shakespeare I read, and Spencer, and the Elizabethans, and Shelley and Keats. I read "Thou still unravished bride of quietness" and found a still water withal strong and potent, quiet with its own strength, and satisfying as bread. That beautiful awareness, so sure of its own power that it is not necessary to create the illusion of force by frenzy and motion. Take the odes to a Nightingale, to a Grecian urn, "Music to hear," etc.; here is the spiritual beauty which the moderns strive vainly for with trickery, and yet beneath it one knows are entrails; masculinity.

Occasionally I see modern verse in magazines. In four years I have found but one cause for interest; a tendency among them to revert to formal rhymes and conventional forms again. Have they, too, seen the writing on the wall? Can one still hope? Or is this age, this decade, impossible for the creation of poetry? Is there nowhere among us a Keats in embryo, someone who will tune his lute to the beauty of the world? Life is not different from what it was when Shelley drove like a swallow southward from the unbearable English winter; living may be different, but not life. Time changes us, but Time's self does not change. Here is the same air, the same sunlight in which Shelly dreamed of golden men and women immortal in a silver world and in which young John Keats wrote "Endymion" trying to gain enough silver to marry Fannie Brawne and set up an apothecary's shop. Is not there among us someone who can write something beautiful and passionate and sad instead of saddening?

William Faulkner.

Oxford, Mississippi.
October, 1924.